BUILDING
CHURCHES
THAT LAST

BUILDING CHURCHES THAT LAST

DISCOVER THE PATTERN FOR NEW TESTAMENT CHURCH GROWTH

Dick Iverson

BY DICK IVERSON
WITH LARRY ASPLUND

A **MANNAHOUSE** RESOURCE

PUBLISHED BY MANNAHOUSE RESOURCE

9200 NE Fremont, Portland, Oregon 97220

Mannahouse Resource is a ministry of Mannahouse and is dedicated to serving the local church and its leaders through the production and distribution of quality materials. It is our prayer that these materials, proven in the context of the local church, will equip leaders in exalting the Lord and extending His kingdom. For a complete listing of resources, please visit our website at www.mannahouseresource.com.

BUILDING CHURCHES THAT LAST

ACKNOWLEDGMENTS

I wish to express my gratitude to the following people without
whom this book would not have been possible:

First, my personal secretary, Roxy Kidder. Thank you
for the innumerable hours you spent developing the
original manuscript.

Second, my dear friend and fellow elder, Larry Asplund. You
gave of yourself without reserve in rewriting the manuscript.
Thank you.

Third, my editor Ben Rigall. My deepest thanks for your final
polishing of the book.

Finally, my dear wife, Edie Iverson. Without your encouragement
this book would not be in our hands. Thanks honey!

✠

FOREWORD

DICK IVERSON IS ONE OF MY FAVORITE PEOPLE. HIS LIFE backs up what he preaches. He's obviously one of God's choice servants, called to touch a city, nation, and the world. His book, *Building Churches That Last,* is must reading for anyone who desires to capture the dynamics of the early church and implement them in his ministry. A pastor's pastor, Iverson writes from extensive experience and outstanding results. He's a veteran pastor who needs to be heard.

As I read the manuscript I realized that many of his principles were the reason God blessed my years of pastoral experience. It was a joy to find a biblical foundation for much of the blessings God bestowed upon us in pastoral ministry.

I commend *Building Churches That Last* to you for careful consideration. It will focus your vision, encourage your heart, and change the way you look at ministry. The truths of his writings need to be understood by the laity as well as clergy. It will help us all understand what true biblical ministry is about.

Joe C. Aldrich
President
Multnomah Bible College
Portland, Oregon

PREFACE

CHURCH GROWTH DRAWS ENORMOUS ATTENTION TODAY. Seminars and conferences focus on it. Books and tapes on the subject flow from publishing houses. I had been in the ministry fifteen years before God opened my eyes to the pattern for church growth. The blueprint spreads across Scripture and must be collected "precept upon precept, line upon line, here a little, there a little" *(Isa. 28:10)*. Once the parts of the blueprint are assembled, it can guide faithful, diligent church leaders.

At the date of this book's publication, I have been in pastoral ministry forty-four years. I started out like many young ministers thinking the church was just a place for Christians to gather, learn Scripture, sing hymns, and pray. I saw the church as a platform for my ministry. I saw it as a place for the preacher — the gifted one — to perform, yet I floundered many years, trying to determine what I was supposed to be doing. I brought in other "noted" ministers to perform, but that only added to my frustration and failure. I felt if the people would only support my leadership, I would be a success, but I had a negative attitude toward the people. I was a shepherd trying to feed sheep I did not love. During those years I was as sincere as I am now, but the Scripture says, "My people are destroyed for lack of knowledge" *(Hos. 4:6)*.

In the mid 1960s the veil began lifting off my eyes. The revelation of *1 Corinthians*, chapter *12*, awakened me. I began seeing the reality of the local body of Christ and how every member was important and was to function in his or her place. I began to see that the church was the instrument of God to extend His kingdom on earth. I began to understand the church as the New Testament house of the Lord.

God rebuked me for my sinful, negative attitude toward His people and birthed in me a great love and appreciation for the body of Christ. For the past thirty years, I have spoken to thousands of leaders around the world delivering portions of this life-message. I have been asked frequently to condense the message into book form. Here it is — a biblical picture of how to build the body of Christ to be a community of overcomers who triumph until the end of time. The reader will not find methods or programs, which must adapt to times, locations, and cultures. However, he or she will find rock-solid, lasting principles around which methods should be built.

We really do not have a choice in the matter. We should not guess how to build God's house, and we do not have to. The pattern is in the Scripture. The best book on church growth was written by the Owner of the church. If we follow the Owner's manual, the Bible, we will succeed in establishing the local church in the community, and we will see it grow according to the New Testament pattern.

I trust this material will provide a plumbline for your life and ministry as you pray that the Lord will "set in order the things that are lacking" where He has placed you. Let us believe the Lord together that He will give us the grace and wisdom to make positive contributions to the church that will be "without spot or wrinkle" when He returns.

— Dick Iverson

CONTENTS

ACKNOWLEDGMENTS v

FOREWORD vii

PREFACE ix

1. The Pattern 1

      The Pattern Church
      Follow the Pattern
      The True Tabernacle
      The Principle of Restoration
      A Church That Will Last
      Distinctives of Church Life

2. The Foundation 17

      The Day of Pentecost
      Repent
      Be Baptized
      Gift of the Holy Spirit
      A Normal Christian Life

3. Added To the Church 37

Born Into the Kingdom
Jesus Started His Church
Adding Believers
Christian Vagabonds
Members of a Body
Selfish Individualism
Membership in the Church
The Planting of the Lord
Kingdom Growth

4. An Apostolic Team 55

Authority in the Old Testament
Authority in the New Testament
Team Ministry
Headship: The Team Leader
Five Leadership Gifts
Restoring Spiritual Authority

5. An Apostolic Fellowship 77

Priority of Doctrine
The Doctrine of Christ
Six Elementary Doctrines
A Life in Common
Relating to One Another

6. A Worshiping Community 95

A Royal Priesthood
The Table of the Lord
Devotion to Prayer
A House of Prayer
Communion in the House
A House of Praise
Davidic Worship
The Glory of the Lord

7. Awesome Signs 119

The Doctrine of Miracles
God Initiates & Man Cooperates
Purpose of Miracles
A Supernaturally Gifted Church
The Fear of the Lord
The Beginning of Wisdom

8. Body Life 141

Life Together
Gifts Require Love
Imbalances Inhibit Life
The Body of Christ
The Mandate to Serve
Changed Hearts
Caring for One Another

9. Assembling Together 159

Unity and Diversity
Cell and Celebration
The Joy of Hospitality

10. Taking the City 175

Uphold Integrity
Light and Leaven
Vision for the City
The Church in the City
Multiplication Yields Fruit

Notes 193

1
The Pattern

*Our fathers had the tabernacle of witness in
the wilderness, as He appointed, instructing
Moses to make it according to the pattern
that he had seen.* — Acts 7:44

S TARRY NIGHT SKIES BOAST OF A DIVINE ORDER IN THE universe. Planets criss-crossthe heavens in charted paths. They move precisely and predictably. Astronomers know exactly where each one will travel. Men can set their watches by the movement. Every visible star obeys the order God built into His creation.

God is not the author of confusion and disorder but of peace and wholeness *(1 Cor. 14:33)*. Order and harmony are in His nature, and anything that is truly of God reflects His divine order. Intricate details in the balance of nature testify that God created the earth to function in order. When examined closely, even things that appear at first to occur at random or by chance have an exact pattern.

God placed mankind at the highest level of creation. He uniquely created man in God's own image. Everything about man shows an astounding intricacy that also reflects the order of God. God marvelously fashioned the human body by divine design. Even the human soul reflects the nature of God.

The Old Testament nation of Israel received the Mosaic Law to establish order in the nation's civil and ceremonial affairs. Priests and the people had to follow precise instructions when approaching the

Lord to worship. God commanded Moses to build a tabernacle in the wilderness "according to the pattern which was shown you on the mountain" *(Exod. 25:40)*. He did not allow the Israelites to stray off and build according to their own design. He did not permit them to follow tangents. God said, "Just make it the way I tell you. Don't do it your own way or take short cuts." Faithfulness to the pattern held supreme significance because at the tabernacle God said He would dwell, meet, and speak with His people *(Exod. 29:42–46)*.

Likewise, in New Testament times Jesus said, "I will build my church," a spiritual temple for a habitation of God in the Spirit *(Matt. 16:18; Eph. 2:21–22)*. As Jesus builds His church, does He have a plan, blueprint or pattern? God required Moses to follow a pattern while building the tabernacle, but is He less careful about the design of the church? Does Jesus just *ad-lib* and react as needs arise, or does God have a divine blueprint for ordering His church in this generation? Fortunately, He did leave a pattern.

THE PATTERN CHURCH

Jesus said He would build His church, and the book of *Acts* shows Him doing it. Acts preserves the history of life in the first New Testament church. Written by Luke, it gives modem Christians a glimpse of the divine pattern before men had time to mess it up. J. B. Phillips wrote that the reader of the book of *Acts* "is seeing Christianity, the real thing, in action for the first time in human history ... the Church as it was meant to be."[1]

When Jesus began to build the church, His powerful dynamics created explosive growth, resulting in the Gospel touching the known world. The church was born on the Day of Pentecost; it multiplied in the city of Jerusalem; it eventually spread to the Samaritans, to a Roman centurion and to the Greeks in Antioch. Starting in Jerusalem and ending in Rome, the church of Jesus Christ quickly established a beachhead in the Roman empire. Although it did not escape every problem — members had disagreements and doctrinal differences-it profoundly impacted its generation with truth and purity.

The principles Jesus uses to build His church are universal and timeless. While methods and programs may vary, principles work in every generation and culture of the world. It is just as important for church leaders and lay ministers today to build "according to the pattern" as it was for Moses. The tabernacle Moses built was a pattern or symbol of the complete plan that was being progressively revealed. The New Testament presents the church as the fulfillment in time and space of the Old Testament pattern.

FOLLOW THE PATTERN

Moses was instructed, "And see to it that you make them [tabernacle furniture] according to the pattern which was shown you on the mountain" *(Exod. 25:40)*. The Bible records this phrase, or variations of it, nine times in reference to the house of God. To be mentioned nine times, the pattern must be very important to God. He is very interested in how things are done in His house.

> *And you shall raise up the tabernacle according to its pattern which you were shown on the mountain.* *(Exod. 26:30)*

> *You shall make it hollow with boards; as it was shown you on the mountain, so shall they make it.* *(Exod. 27:8)*

> *According to all that I show you, that is, the pattern of the tabernacle and the pattern of all its furnishings, just so you shall make it.* *(Exod. 25:9)*

> *According to all that I have commanded you, they shall do.* *(Exod. 31:11)*

And the children of Israel did according to all that the LORD had
commanded Moses; so they did. (Exod. 39:32, 42, 43)

According to the pattern which the LORD had shown Moses,
so he made. (Num. 8:4)

Disharmony had marred creation in the first place due to man's independence and rebellion. Therefore, God required His people to set aside their independence and faithfully follow His lead. It was absolutely necessary. Any generation that refused to follow God's pattern ended in death and destruction. *(See Josh. 22:28; 2 Kings 16:10; 1 Chron. 28:11, 12, 18, 19; Ezek. 43:10)*. Israel obeyed the Lord's instruction and built ACCORDING TO THE PATTERN.

The New Testament deacon, Stephen, was martyred shortly after he testified before the synagogue council. He had referred to the Old Testament story of Moses and the tabernacle pattern.

Our fathers had the tabernacle of witness in the wilderness, as he
appointed, instructing Moses to make it according to the pattern
that he had seen. (Acts 7:44)

Stephen pointed out that God had directed the construction and daily operation of the house of the Lord by revelation. It was God's house, and He wanted it built according to His design. In addition, Stephen referred to the Israelites who had lived around the tabernacle for forty years as the symbolic "church in the wilderness" *(Acts 7:38)*. He reminded his listeners that their forefathers' constant rebellion had forced them to wander in the wilderness until a whole generation died — even though they traveled in the presence of the tabernacle. Today the church wanders in a wilderness of conflicting opinions, traditions, habits, and man-made patterns searching for the presence of the Lord "though He is not far from ... us" *(Acts 17:27)*.

God was explicit with Moses about the pattern for the tabernacle because it was a shadow of the true tabernacle, which the Lord would build later.

> [a] *copy and shadow of heavenly things, as Moses was divinely instructed when he was about to make the tabernacle. For He said, "See that you make all things according to the pattern shown you on the mountain."*   (Heb. 8:5 emphasis added)

> *A Minister of the sanctuary and of the true tabernacle which the Lord erected, and not man.*   (Heb. 8:2 emphasis added)

THE TRUE TABERNACLE

The true tabernacle — the true house of the Lord — is the church Jesus is building.

> *Who was faithful to Him who appointed Him, as Moses also was faithful in all his house. For this One has been counted worthy of more glory than Moses, inasmuch as He who built the house has more honor than the house. For every house is built by someone, but He who built all things is God. And Moses indeed was faithful in all His house as a servant, for a testimony of those things which would be spoken afterward, but Christ as a Son over His own house, whose house we are if we hold fast the confidence and the rejoicing of the hope firm to the end.*   (Heb. 3:2–6 emphasis added)

If the tabernacle in the wilderness had to be built according to God's pattern, how much more must the true tabernacle be built according to the New Testament pattern. Today more than 400 books about church growth crowd the shelves of Christian bookstores. They tell how to target areas according to demographics, how to promote churches, how to conduct services, and how to do whatever it takes to see a church grow. In other words, they attempt to show ministers how to build the church. Few of these books say, "Let's go back to the New Testament and build according to the pattern."

The apostle Paul followed a spiritual blueprint or pattern. First, he laid the foundation, and then he built on it. He wrote:

> *For we are God's fellow workers; you are God's field, you are God's building. According to the grace of God which was given to me, as a wise master builder I have laid the foundation.*
>
> *(1 Cor. 3:9–10).*

> *But let each one take heed how he builds on it. For no other foundation can anyone lay than that which is laid, which is Jesus Christ.*
>
> *(1 Cor. 3:10–11)*

Christian believers are God's building; however, they also are the Lord's fellow builders. From the foundation up, builders must build the right way, according to the pattern. Paul warned every builder to "take heed how he builds." Paul himself worked to keep God's order in the church. He said,

> *Let all things be done decently and in order.*   *(1 Cor. 14:40 KJV)*

> *For though I be absent in the flesh, yet am I with you in the spirit, joying and beholding your order, and the stedfastness of your faith in Christ.*   *(Col. 2:5 KJV)*

> *For this cause left I thee in Crete, that thou shouldest set in order the things that are wanting, and ordain elders in every city, as I had appointed thee.*   *(Titus 1:5 KJV)*

THE PRINCIPLE OF RESTORATION

Today God is restoring his church to the same life and power that enabled Christianity to become a world religion in one generation. The principle of restoration is one of the most foundational in all of Scripture. It rests on the belief that God's original works reveal unblemished patterns or blueprints in creation. It also assumes that fallen, sinful man tends to stray from the original pattern over time. As man strays, he loses his life and he needs restoration.

The principle appears first in Genesis. In the beginning when man sinned, he lost all God originally had intended for him. He lost his fellowship with God, and as a sinner he could not fulfill his original, God-given purpose. But God immediately made a way for mankind to be reconciled and restored. The Lord established the plan of redemption.

> *And I will put enmity between you and the woman, and between your seed and her Seed; He shall bruise your head, and you shall bruise His heel.* (Gen. 3:15)

> *Also for Adam and his wife the Lord God made tunics of skin, and clothed them.* (Gen. 3:21)

The Mosaic Law instituted restoration into civil regulations of the land. It required the return of stolen goods to their owners — with interest.

> *If a man steals an ox or a sheep, and slaughters it or sells it, he shall restore five oxen for an ox and four sheep for a sheep.* (Exod. 22:1)

If fire breaks out and catches in thorns, so that stacked grain, standing grain, or the field is consumed, he who kindled the fire shall surely make restitution.   *(Exod. 22:6)*

King Solomon echoed the principle in his wisdom writings.

People do not despise a thief if he steals to satisfy himself when he is starving. Yet when he is found, he must restore sevenfold.
(Prov. 6:30–31)

Adam and Eve had enjoyed God's perfect order in the earth until they sinned. Later, the church followed a similar path. The church was born following an original visitation of the Holy Spirit. The visitation revealed God's original design for the church. Truth and power characterized life among first-century believers. However, soon human pride and sin led Christians astray from the God-given pattern. As a result they lost the life they enjoyed and needed restoration.

The church was just newly born when Peter preached about the end of its history. Between the beginning and the end, believers would enjoy times of refreshing as a result of their faith in Christ *(Acts 3:19)*. Eventually Jesus would return for His bride. Peter said Jesus would return only after all things spoken of by the prophets had been restored

... Jesus Christ, who was preached to you before, whom heaven must receive until the times of restoration of all things, which God has spoken by the mouth of all His holy prophets since the world began.
(Acts 3:20–21)

The Bible declares that God is restoring His church, and that He will continue to restore it until it is the glorious bride of Christ

... that He might present it to Himself a glorious church, not having spot or wrinkle or any such thing, but that it should be holy and without blemish   *(Eph. 5:27)*

If God is restoring the church, and if the church will conform to the glorious pattern, then discovering the pattern becomes absolutely essential.

Humanists view man as his own god and believe man is perfectible without God's help. They think humanity is progressing over time and that things continue to improve as a result of new discoveries and achievements. They do not recognize designs or patterns in origins. They assume everything began in a primitive form and steadily gets better on its own. They see no need for restoration of things that get better by themselves.[2]

Many, even in the church, have been trained by educators, the media, and politicians to think like humanists. If they believe the church is automatically progressing, getting better over time, then restoring an original pattern is irrelevant to them.

I am convinced that before the return of the Lord, the church will be restored according to God's design!

A CHURCH THAT WILL LAST

When Jesus said, "I will build My church," he went on to say, "the gates of Hades shall not prevail against it" *(Matt. 16:18)*. The church Jesus is building is an overcoming, triumphant church. His statement implies that if a church does not conform to His pattern, then He is not building it and the gates of hell will prevail against it.

The apostle Paul warned church leaders to take heed how they build. Jesus is the foundation, but Paul said that not everything built on the foundation will last.

Now if anyone builds on this foundation with gold, silver, precious stones, wood, hay, straw. (1 Cor. 3:12)

A house of gold, silver, and precious stones will endure, while a house of wood, hay, and straw will not last. For that reason every church or house of God will be tested. Fiery trials reveal the true qualities of each house.

Each one's work will become manifest; for the Day will declare it, because it will be revealed by fire; and the fire will test each one's work, of what sort it is. (1 Cor. 3:13)

A house built according to the pattern will last.

If anyone's work which he has built on it endures, he will receive a reward. If anyone's work is burned, he will suffer loss; but he himself will be saved, yet so as through fire. (I Cor. 3:14–15)

The Builder wants His co-laborers to use eternal building materials and to follow the pattern He has revealed. All who study God's pattern must commit themselves to use it. True leaders long for the church to reflect God's pattern and purpose. Every leader with a shepherd's heart wants the dynamics of the church to be ordered by the Lord. No one has the right or freedom to build the church in his or her own way. No one has the right to decide what it should be like, how it should operate, its mission and lifestyle. Moses had no choice how he was to build and neither do we.

Programs do not always build a house of gold, silver, and precious stones. They are important and may benefit the church but they are not the essence, dynamic, or purpose of the church. They certainly do not make the church alive. They are often additions to the house. They are rooms in the house at best.

Adjustments will be necessary, and everyone has to be willing to make adjustments to build according to the pattern. Throughout their lives, individual Christians have to make adjustments. As they do, their vision gets clearer. They see God's pattern for their lives more fully than before. If they are wise, they will make whatever adjustments might be called for by the Spirit and the Word.

If believers are not teachable, they will not see and understand the Lord's pattern for the church. If they do not grasp the pattern, they surely will not implement it. An unteachable person says, "I have done it this way for 30 years, and I will continue to do it this way until I die." That is the way to death.

DISTINCTIVES OF CHURCH LIFE

The book of *Acts* contains more than history. It is the second half of a two-volume Gospel. Luke wrote the books to reinforce his readers' faith. As he narrates history he also teaches theology.[3] He explains the dynamics of the first New Testament church and illustrates the principles.

His first volume, the Gospel of Luke, covers Jesus' life and teachings. Acts follows what the Holy Spirit continued to do and teach in Jesus' name through the church. Opening statements in both volumes reveal Luke's purpose:

> *Inasmuch as many have taken in hand to set in order a narrative those things which are most surely believed among us, just as those who from the beginning were eyewitnesses and ministers of the word delivered them to us, it seemed good to me also, having had perfect understanding of all things from the very first, to write to you an orderly account, most excellent Theophilus, that you may know the certainty of those things in which you were instructed*
> (*Luke 1:1–4* emphasis added)

The former account I made, O Theophilus, of all that Jesus began both to do and teach, until the day in which He was taken up, after He through the Holy Spirit had given commandments to the apostles whom He had chosen, to whom He also presented Himself alive after His suffering by many infallible proofs, being seen by them during forty days and speaking of the things pertaining to the kingdom of God. (Acts 1:1–3)

Luke's readers needed to know with certainty that what they were believing and doing had been started by Jesus and continued by the Holy Spirit. Their faith in Jesus and their experience of the body of Jesus needed to be founded on an authoritative, orderly witness. Luke provided it for them — and for churchmen and women today.

The Jerusalem church is the first fulfillment of Jesus' promise in *Matt. 16:18.* For several years, the church faithfully followed the pattern, although it had an advantage over many churches today. All the converts had the same ethnic heritage. As Jews, they shared a background in Old Testament Scripture. It enabled them to correctly apply the teachings of Christ and the leading of the Holy Spirit. Modern-day believers often have difficulty correctly applying the teachings of Christ without the context of Old Testament Scripture.

Acts 2:38–47; 4:31–35, and *5:12–16* describe the distinctives of the early church. The same distinctives should be explored and implemented in local churches today. These distinctives show:

- The New Testament church had a clear doctrinal and experiential foundation. It began with repentance, demonstrated by an initial experience of baptism. It was then energized and controlled by the Holy Spirit.

- Converts immediately identified with the community of believers. They did not become spiritual "Lone Rangers." Those who responded to the preached Word recognized a covenant relationship with one another as a logical part of their covenant with the Lord.

- A leadership structure of apostles and elders governed the community of faith. The twelve apostles appointed by the Lord composed the original leadership team. With the leading of the Holy Spirit, they did not hesitate to exercise the authority the Lord delegated to them.

- Believers entered into a new lifestyle almost immediately — a pattern of receiving and living according to the instruction of the apostles. As a result, they lived together in a vibrant fellowship.

- Given to prayer and praise, the New Testament church was a worshiping community in love with the Lord. Christians visibly celebrated His Lordship.

- The presence and power of Christ was evident. The Lord confirmed the preached Word with miraculous signs and wonders. The supernatural events brought the fear of the Lord upon believers as well as upon their neighbors and onlookers.

- Members took fellowship seriously and expressed it practically. They lived a lifestyle of selfless service, living out the dynamic of the cross.

- Believers maintained unity. They assembled together at various places and times for worship, instruction, and for simply sharing their lives together.

- Neighbors and people in surrounding areas were impressed by the markedly different life in the Christian community. Many chose to believe the Gospel and became part of the remarkable community.

The pattern demonstrated in the book of *Acts* is still the pattern for the church. The Lord is restoring and building His church according to the same principles and dynamics. They hold true today and will continue in every generation. The closer we come to the return of the Lord, the more we will experience in our own lives and churches the living reality of the dynamics of the New Testament church.

Begin now to study the pattern, believe it, contend for it, and to believe God for the wisdom to implement it. ✠

STUDY QUESTIONS

1. Why is it important to understand that God is orderly?

2. How important is God's pattern? Why?

3. How important is God's building pattern to the church? Why?

4. How can God's pattern be seen in the book of *Acts*?

5. What is the principle of restoration?

6. How does the principle of restoration relate to God's pattern in the church?

7. What kind of church will Jesus return to claim?

8. Therefore, how should the church be built?

9. What is the significance of the picture of the church recorded in *Acts*, chapter *2*?

10. How is the picture of the church in *Acts*, chapter *2*, relevant to the church today?

2 The Foundation

"Repent, and let everyone of you be baptized in the name of Jesus Christ for the remission of sins; and you shall receive the gift of the Holy Spirit. For the promise is to you, and to your children, and to all who are afar off, as many as the Lord our God will call." And with many other words he testified and exhorted them, saying, "Be saved from this perverse generation". — Acts 2:38–40

THE FOUNDATION OF New Covenant life begins with repentance. Humble, repentant believers then follow Christ's example and the apostles' clear teaching to be baptized. Finally, they receive power to live triumphant Christian lives by receiving the gift of the Holy Spirit.

A house rests on the strength of its foundation. The one who builds a strong foundation will build a strong house. Today more than ever, Christians must build their lives carefully according to the pattern of God's Word. Without strong foundations, they limit the size and scope of how largely they can build. If they do not build according to the pattern, their building will have cracks, crumble, and fall.

After preaching his Sermon on the Mount, Jesus illustrated the importance of building a solid foundation:

Therefore whoever hears these sayings of Mine, and does them, I will liken him to a wise man who built his house on the rock; and the house; and it did not fall, for it was founded on the rock. Now everyone who hears these sayings of Mine, and does not do them, will be like a foolish man who built his house on the sand: and the rain descended, the floods came, and the winds blew and beat on that house; and it fell. And great was its fall. (Matt. 7:24–27)

Acts, chapter 2, chronicles the birth of the first church in simplicity and power. The biblical account has preserved the design of the church's foundation. The chapter also describes the foundation of individual Christian lives. It gives a clear pattern for coming to God, knowing Him as Lord and Savior, knowing His ways, and walking in victory. It illustrates how converts become fruitful members of the church.

The first church's solid foundation allowed it to fulfill the commission to extend the kingdom of God. This pioneer group of believers carried the Gospel to the farthest parts of the Roman empire, including the capitol city of Rome.

THE DAY OF PENTECOST

The apostle Peter first announced the foundation's blueprint on the Day of Pentecost, fifty days after Christ's death, burial and resurrection. The Feast of Pentecost was also called the Feast of Weeks or the Feast of Harvest in the Old Testament *(Exod. 23:16; 34:22; Lev. 23:15–22; Num. 28:26; Deut. 16:10,16)*. It was one of three major religious events in Israel's sacred calendar.

The feast celebrated the giving of the Law at Mount Sinai and the birth of natural Israel as a covenant nation. Now, on natural Israel's anniversary, spiritual Israel, the church, was born as the New Covenant nation *(See 1 Pet. 2:9)*.

The feast drew large crowds. Devout Jews from all over the world as well as proselytes to Judaism attended it. Acts lists people from fifteen nations and regions. At 9:00 in the morning thousands of them heard strange sounds coming from a house. Amazed and perplexed, they stopped to inquire. While some mocked, Peter stood up — perhaps on an upper balcony — and preached his first sermon under the inspiration of the Holy Spirit.

Peter pointed to Christ's supernatural life and ministry, which had been seen by people who lived in Jerusalem. He used *Ps. 16:8–11* to support his claim that Jesus is the Messiah who rose from the dead. Then he declared:

> *This Jesus God has raised up, of which we are all witnesses. Therefore being exalted to the right hand of God, and having received from the Father the promise of the Holy Spirit, He poured out this which you now see and hear.* (Acts 2:32–33)

The resurrected, exalted Messiah, Jesus of Nazareth, was now pouring out the Holy Spirit on all flesh as the Father had promised through the prophet Joel *(Joel 2:28–32)*. The New Covenant age, the age of the Holy Spirit, had dawned upon the world. Anxiety and remorse mixed with sharp pain to humble about 3,000 people. They were cut to the heart because of what they had done. Prophecy had been fulfilled in Jesus, the Messiah, whom they had rejected and crucified, and now they were convicted.

> *Now when they heard this, they were cut to the heart, and said to Peter and the rest of the apostles, "Men and brethren, what shall we do?"* (Acts 2:37)

A new day had come and a New Covenant offered salvation. Peter gave everyone hearing the news about the earth-shaking offer a chance to respond to it. He called everyone within the sound of his voice to lay the New Covenant foundation in their lives. He called them to repent, get baptized, and receive the gift of the Holy Spirit *(Acts 2:38)*.

REPENT

The word *repent* or *repentance* is used about sixty times in the New Testament. The Greek word for repentance is *metánoia*. It originally meant an afterthought — a second thought that revealed the error of the first thought. *Metánoia* refers to a change of mind and feeling or a change of principle and practice to reverse the past. It is a change of inner values that results in a change of action.

A. T. Robertson paraphrases Peter's words as follows: "**Change your mind and your life**. Turn right about and do it now. You *crucified* this Jesus. Now *crown* Him in your hearts as Lord and Christ."[4]

Charles Finney defined repentance as "changing your mind from what you have believed on any given subject to what God has revealed on that subject." Instead of going by their own ideas and interpretations, believers are to think God's thoughts on every subject. Faulty thinking leads to wrong behavior.

Repent is the first word of the Gospel.   John the Baptist's message began with a command to repent.

> *In those days John the Baptist came preaching in the wilderness of Judea, and saying, "Repent, for the kingdom of heaven is at hand!"*
> *(Matt. 3:1–2)*

Repent was the first word in the message of Jesus.

> *From that time Jesus began to preach and to say, "Repent, for the kingdom of heaven is at hand."*   *(Matt. 4:17)*

New Testament apostles preached repentance.

Repent therefore and be converted, that your sins may be blotted out, so that times of refreshing may come from the presence of the Lord. (Acts 3:19; see also 8:22)

Truly, these times of ignorance God overlooked, but now commands all men every where to repent. (Acts 17:30)

The New Testament concludes with a call to repent.

Remember therefore from where you have fallen; repent and do the first works, or else I will come to you quickly and remove your lampstand from its place — unless you repent.
(Rev. 2:5; see also 2:16, 21, 22)

Remember therefore how you have received and heard; hold fast and repent. (Rev. 3:3; see also 3:19)

Old Testament prophets preached repentance.

"They said, 'Repent now everyone of his evil way and his evil doings, and dwell in the land that the LORD has given to you and your fathers forever and ever.'" (Jer. 25:5)

"Therefore say to the house of Israel, 'Thus says the Lord GOD: "Repent, turn away from your idols, and turn your faces away from all your abominations."'" (Ezek. 14:6; see also 18:30)

Repentance affects the past and the future. It brings grief or sorrow for improper conduct and the faulty thinking behind it *(2 Cor. 7:9)*. Repentance involves an actual turning away from bad conduct *(Acts 8:22)* and a turning to a new way of thinking *(Mark 1:15)*.

Forgiveness covers sins of the past, and a changed mind and heart lead to a healthy future.

A vital, healthy life requires acknowledgement of sin and wrongdoing. In today's technological society, people are told to do everything except repent. They are told to explain situations away, blame someone else, accentuate the positive, or attribute failures to heredity and environment. The fact remains that the only way to deal with sin and its consequences is through repentance.

Repentance is not just an emotional response. It means people have heard God's Word and discovered that their thinking has been contrary to His Word. When they decide to change their thinking to conform to God's thinking, they have repented. When they find God's revealed truth on any subject, they repent and change their minds to conform to God's mind (See *Luke 7:29 NIV; John 3:33; 2 Thess. 1:5*). It is a radical change of mind, away from sin and self and toward God.

Repentance is not just the conviction of sin. Godly sorrow precedes repentance. The Holy Spirit caused listeners in Jerusalem to be "cut to the heart" *(Acts 2:37)*. They were convicted of their sin but had not yet repented. People may be in a worship service, in the presence of the Lord, and their hearts are pricked. They realize their sinfulness before a holy God and may even find a way to express those feelings. But if they walk out without changing their thinking and the direction of their lives and continue to do whatever the Lord has convicted them of, they certainly did not repent. False repentance is a self-centered sorrow over the consequences of sin.

Repentance is not just reformation. Repentance involves reformation because a truly repentant person will turn around and start over in demonstratable ways. However, if God is not involved in the reformation, and if reformation is not based on the work of the Cross, then it is not repentance and ultimately it will fail. The determination to do better, "turning over a new leaf," and self-help programs do not constitute repentance.

Repentance is not just being religious.   Many people think they must act religious if they repent, so they learn religious jargon, a religious pose, and a religious tone of voice. Anyone can go through the motions, attend a dynamic local church, learn praise choruses, raise his hands, shout "Hallelujah," and still not repent.

Repentance is not "only believism."   Repentance is more than a new mental attitude. It is more than accepting the truth about Jesus and His kingdom. True repentance always includes a transformation of the entire life of the individual. It leads to observable changes in his or her life. John the Baptist expected to see evidence of repentance. He said: *Therefore bear fruits worthy of repentance .... He who has two tunics, let him give to him who has none; and he who has food, let him do likewise. ... Collect no more than what is appointed for you. ... Do not intimidate anyone or accuse falsely, and be content with your wages (Luke 3:8, 11, 13, 14).*

Repentance focuses on the root of sin — the attitude behind sin — and not on a specific sin. The repentant person must focus on the condition of his heart before a holy God. He must be more than sorry for the rotten fruit in his life — that he got drunk or committed fornication.

An unrepentant person is committed to going his own way and doing his own thing apart from God. Jeremiah said, *"The heart is deceitful above all things, and desperately wicked; who can know it?"* (Jer. 17:9). Isaiah agrees: *"All we like sheep have gone astray; we have turned, every one, to his own way"* (Isa. 53:6).

True repentance is based on the recognition that man has sinned against God and has broken fellowship with Him.   Peter preached to law keepers on the Day of Pentecost. They were trying to follow the Mosaic Law and keep the Judaism of their day. But the root of their sin was the fact that they had rejected Jesus Christ. They devoted their lives to studying the Old Testament, but they rejected the One who fulfilled the Old Testament. When Peter preached the Gospel to them, they realized they had sinned and were separated from God. It is no wonder they said, "What shall we do?"

True repentance recognizes human responsibility to turn from sin. The Gospel must turn men and women from the sin of unbelief. After agreeing with the Gospel and trusting Christ for salvation, new believers must begin lives of simple obedience.

Why must people repent? Following are eight reasons:

1. God commands people to repent. It is not an option. His commandment is immediate and universal. *"God ... commands all men every where to repent" (Acts 17:30).*

2. Christ came into the world to call all men to repentance, and everyone will be judged by his or her response to Christ's call. *"I have not come to call the righteous, but sinners, to repentance" (Luke 5:32).*

3. Repentance guides people away from destruction. *"Unless you repent you will all likewise perish" (Luke 13:3, 5).* A man may be sincere. He may be morally good, but if he is not in full agreement with God's truth, if he does not rely on Christ alone for salvation and righteousness, then he is a sinner, separated from God and headed for destruction.

4. Forgiveness hinges on repentance. *"If your brother sins against you, rebuke him; and if he repents, forgive him" (Luke 17:3).* Notice repentance occurs first, then forgiveness can follow.

5. Repentance qualifies people to enter the kingdom of God. *"Repent, for the kingdom of heaven is at hand" (Matt. 4:17).* The kingdom of God is within reach, but the only way to enter is through repentance.

6. God desires that all men repent. *"The Lord is not slack concerning His promise, as some count slackness, but is longsuffering toward us, not willing that any should perish but that all should come to repentance" (2 Pet. 3:9).* God's heart longs for all men everywhere to repent, turn to Him, and receive His life.

7. Repentance leads to life. *"When they heard these things they became silent; and they glorified God, saying, 'Then God has also granted to the Gentiles repentance to life'" (Acts 11:18).* Repentance does not lead to bondage. Turning to Jesus produces true life.

8. Repentance makes true faith possible. The words *repentance* and *faith* often appear together in the Bible. People repent so they can become connected with God. They repent so they can believe. Jesus Christ calls people to repentance because He wants them to place their faith in Him, to come to know Him and to receive His life.

> *... testifying both to Jews, and also to Greeks, repentance toward God and faith toward our Lord Jesus Christ.* (Acts 20:21)

> *The time is fulfilled, and the kingdom of God is at hand. Repent, and believe in the gospel.* (Mark 1:15; see also Heb. 6:1)

> *Him God has exalted to His right hand to be Prince and Savior, to give repentance to Israel and forgiveness of sins.* (Acts 5:31)

BE BAPTIZED

Baptism in water is the initial sign that a person has repented and believed in Jesus. The New Testament refers to it as the "baptism of repentance" *(Luke 3:3)*. Baptism reveals an obedient attitude toward Christ and His Word. *"... baptism, not the removal of the filth of the flesh, but the answer of a good conscience toward God"* (1 Pet. 3:21). A person who really has repented will not say, "I know Jesus has commanded me to be baptized, but I'm not ready to do it yet. I'll get around to it some day. It's really not that important." When a person repents, he agrees with God, including what God has said about baptism.

The Williams *New Testament* translates *Acts 2:38* as follows: *"You must repent — and, as an expression of it, let every one of you be baptized in the name of Jesus Christ — that you may have your sins forgiven."*[5]

While Peter commanded all of his listeners as a group to repent, he charged them as individuals to be baptized. "Let each one of you be baptized," he said. Each one of them had to determine whether to enter into covenant relationship with Jesus Christ. Each one had to make his own decision.

Jesus set the pattern by insisting on His own baptism when He announced His New Covenant mission.

> *Then Jesus came from Galilee to John at the Jordan to be baptized by him. And John tried to prevent Him, saying, "I need to be baptized by You, and are You coming to me?" But Jesus answered and said to him, "Permit it to be so now, for thus it is fitting for us to fulfill all righteousness." Then he allowed Him.*   *(Matt. 3:13–15)*

Water baptism is the sign of the New Covenant.   Baptism is to the New Covenant what circumcision was to the old covenant. It is the outward sign that someone has entered into a covenant relationship with the Lord. "For as many of you as were baptized into Christ have put on Christ" *(Gal. 3:27)*.

> *For he is not a Jew who is one outwardly, nor is circumcision that which is outward in the flesh; but he is a Jew who is one inwardly; and circumcision is that of the heart, in the Spirit, not in the letter; whose praise is not from men but from God.*   *(Rom. 2:28–29)*

Peter declared converts must be baptized "in the name of Jesus Christ." Baptism in the name of Jesus means "to the account of Jesus" or "with reference to Jesus." To be baptized in Christ's name means by His authority, acknowledging His claims, subscribing to His doctrines, engaging in His service, and relying on His merits. At baptism, a believer enters an alliance with Jesus.

The pattern in Acts shows baptism consistently followed repentance

> *Then those who gladly received his word were baptized.*
>   *(Acts 2:41; see also 8:12)*

> *Now as they went down the road, they came to some water. And the eunuch said, 'See, here is water. What hinders me from being baptized?' Then Philip said, 'If you believe with all your heart, you may.' And he answered and said, 'I believe that Jesus Christ is the Son of God.' So he commanded the chariot to stand still. And both Philip and the eunuch went down into the water, and he baptized him.*   *(Acts 8:36–38; see also 9:18)*

> *"Can anyone forbid water, that these should not be baptized who have received the Holy Spirit just as we have?" And he commanded them to be baptized in the name of the Lord.*
>   *(Acts 10:47–48; see also 16:15, 32–33)*

> *And now why are you waiting? Arise and be baptized, and wash away your sins, calling on the name of the Lord.* (Acts 22:16)

Water baptism delivers a benefit of forgiveness of sins. "Be baptized in the name of Jesus Christ for the remission of sins" *(Acts 2:38)*. The word *remission* means strongly dismissed, delivered from captivity, forgiven, pardoned. Forgiveness comes as a result of repentance, which is symbolized by baptism. Repentance and baptism release converts from sin. Believers receive grace to overcome sin.[6]

Paul pointed out the significance of baptism in dealing with sin. The following passages best illustrate his understanding.

> *Or do you not know that as many of us as were baptized into Christ Jesus were baptized into His death? Therefore we were buried with Him through baptism into death, that just as Christ was raised from the dead by the glory of the Father, even so we also should walk in newness of life.* (Rom. 6:3–4)

> *In Him you were also circumcised with the circumcision made without hands, by putting off the body of the sins of the flesh, by the circumcision of Christ, buried with Him in baptism, in which you also were raised with Him through faith in the working of God, who raised Him from the dead. And you, being dead in your trespasses and the uncircumcision of your flesh, He has made alive together with Him, having forgiven you all trespasses.* (Col. 2:11–13)

GIFT OF THE HOLY SPIRIT

One benefit of repentance is forgiveness. Another benefit is the gift of the Holy Spirit. When he declared "you will receive the gift of the Holy Spirit," Peter meant that the person of the Holy Spirit is the gift.

Peter used *dōreá,* a general word for gift, and not *charísma,* the word used in *1 Corinthians,* chapter 12, to refer to the nine gifts of the Spirit.

Before the Day of Pentecost, John the Baptist's ministry featured repentance and water baptism. The fullness of the Holy Spirit in believers' lives made the New Covenant inaugurated by Christ truly unique and powerful.

In Old Testament times, God had anointed certain individuals with miraculous powers of the Holy Spirit. The Holy Spirit came upon prophets, priests, and kings *(I Kings 19:15–16)* or filled them temporarily to accomplish certain tasks. Moses thought the anointing of the Holy Spirit was such a blessing that he yearned for the day when all God's people would receive it *(Num. 11:29).* Through the prophets, God the Father promised to send the Holy Spirit to dwell permanently inside His people.

The prophets declared:

When the Lord has washed away the filth of the daughters of Zion, and purged the blood of Jerusalem from her midst, by the spirit of judgment and by the spirit of burning. (Isa. 4:4; see also 32:15; 44:3)

I will give you a new heart and put a new spirit within you; I will take the heart of stone out of your flesh and give you a heart of flesh. I will put My Spirit within you and cause you to walk in My statutes, and you will keep My judgments and do them
(Ezek. 36:26–27; see also 11:19).

And it shall come to pass afterward that I will pour out My Spirit upon all flesh; your sons and your daughters will prophecy, your old men shall dream dreams, your young men shall see visions; and also on My menservants and on My maidservants I will pour out my Spirit in those days! (Joel 2:28–29)

Peter boldly declared to his audience on the Day of Pentecost that these prophecies were being fulfilled in their midst. Jesus had promised His disciples a new and living relationship with the Holy Spirit following His death and resurrection. Now the Messiah was introducing this new dimension of the Spirit, and it would include greater intimacy with the Father and the Son.

> *He who believes in Me, as the Scripture has said, out of his heart will flow rivers of living water. But this He spoke concerning the Spirit, whom those believing in Him would receive; for the Holy Spirit was not yet given, because Jesus was not yet glorified.*
> *(John 7:38–39)*

> *And I will pray the Father, and He will give you another Helper, that He may abide with you forever, the Spirit of truth, whom the world cannot receive, because it neither sees Him nor knows Him; but you know Him, for He dwells with you and will be in you.*
> *(John 14:16–17; see also 14:26; 15:26–27; 16:13)*

Jesus had told the disciples to wait in Jerusalem until they were endued with God's power. He told them specifically that the power of the Holy Spirit would enable them to be His official witnesses to the ends of the earth.

> *Behold, I send the Promise of My Father upon you; but tarry in the city of Jerusalem until you are endued with power from on high.*
> *(Luke 24:49)*

Before the disciples could fulfill the Great Commission, they had to be filled with the Spirit. It was the only way they would have the power to do the job. They had doubted, and at times the Lord had rebuked them for their lack of faith *(Luke 8:22–25)*. They were ready to call fire down from heaven on all who rejected them *(Luke 9:54)*. Peter had been used as an instrument or mouthpiece for Satan *(Matt. 16:22–23)*. They had fled when Jesus was taken captive *(Mark 14:50)*. Was this the group that Christ was commissioning to go into all the world? Were these the pillars *(Gal. 2:9)* of the New Testament church? For them to influence the world in their generation, the disciples needed to experience the Holy Spirit's divine power themselves.

Both Jesus and John the Baptist had promised a new baptism in the Holy Spirit. To be baptized in the Spirit means the believer is fully immersed in the Spirit.

> *I indeed baptize you with water unto repentance, but He who is coming after me is mightier than I, whose sandals I am not worthy to carry. He will baptize you with the Holy Spirit and fire.*
> *(Matt. 3:11;* see also *Mark 1:8; Luke 3:16; John 1:33)*

> *And being assembled together with them, He commanded them not to depart from Jerusalem, but to wait for the Promise of the Father, "which," He said, "you have heard from Me; for John truly baptized with water, but you shall be baptized with the Holy Spirit not many days from now"* *(Acts 1:4–5).*

Acts refers not only to people being baptized in the Spirit *(1:5; 11:16)* but also to the Holy Spirit *coming upon* them *(1:8; 19:6)*, being *filled* with or *full* of the Spirit *(2:4; 4:8, 31; 6:3, 5; 7:55; 9:17; 11:24; 13:9, 52)*, the Holy Spirit being poured out on them *(2:17, 18, 33; 10:45)*, *receiving* the Holy Spirit *(2:38; 8:15, 17; 10:47; 19:2)*, the Holy Spirit *falling* upon them *(10:44; 11:15)*, and the Holy Spirit being *given* to them *(15:8)*.

Some people suggest the baptism in the Holy Spirit is simply another reference to water baptism. Others suggest it refers to the new birth. Baptism in water and baptism in the Spirit are not the same. The word *baptism* refers to initiation into the covenant. The question is: What is the role of the Holy Spirit in this initiation?

In his commentary, I. Howard Marshall stated:

Just as John's baptism had mediated the divine gift of forgiveness, symbolized in the act of washing, so too Christian baptism was regarded as a sign of forgiveness .... But Christian baptism conveyed an additional blessing. John had said that he baptized (only) with water but the Messiah would baptize with the Holy Spirit, and this gift accompanied water baptism performed by the church in the name of Jesus. The two gifts are closely linked, since it is the Spirit who accomplishes the inner cleansing of which baptism is the outward symbol.[7]

The Holy Spirit takes up residence within people who come to the Lord in true repentance and faith. They become sons of God *(John 1:12)*. Not only does the Spirit come to abide in His people, He comes to fill, saturate, lead, and govern their lives. The Holy Spirit changes the convert, molding him into the character of Christ and drawing others to Christ.

The Bible says the Spirit baptizes and fills believers. In baptism, the Holy Spirit surrounds the believer. Being filled implies that the believer actually contains the Holy Spirit. The Holy Spirit saturates the exterior life and floods the interior life. He gives believers waters to swim in as well as waters flowing out of their lives.

The first Christians were initially baptized in the Spirit and repeatedly filled. Whenever the same believers needed the Holy Spirit's power and guidance, they expected a fresh filling.

And when they had prayed, the place where they were assembled together was shaken; and they were all filled with the Holy Spirit, and they spoke the word of God with boldness. (Acts 4:31)

This was not considered a new or second baptism but a fresh filling of the Spirit. It empowers believers to overcome new obstacles. Being filled with the Spirit launches believers into the supernatural realm with manifestations of the Spirit. The first believers spoke in other tongues when they were filled with the Spirit. Some also prophesied. The supernatural had taken up residence within them. This was the pattern at Jerusalem in *Acts 2:1–4*; at Samaria in *Acts, chapter 8*; with Paul in *Acts 9:17–18*; with Cornelius in *Acts 10:44–47* and *11:15–17*; and at Ephesus in *Acts 19:1–6*.[8]

Christians must have the power of the Holy Spirit. The baptism of the Spirit gives believers inner power, but getting into the realm of the Spirit is not enough. Christians must continually walk under the Spirit's influence. People often draw attention to the initial act of receiving the Spirit without emphasizing the continuing effect on believers' lives. By divorcing the initial experience from continual fillings, people stop short.

On the Day of Pentecost, Peter declared that the promise of the Father was fulfilled. But the fulfillment of the promise extended far beyond that day, he said. The promise was for them, their offspring, and for future generations. It was for all those who are "far off," referring to the Gentiles. Peter also said the promise was for "as many as the Lord our God invites." Whoever the Lord calls receives the promised gift of the Holy Spirit — even today!

Peter continued to address the Pentecost crowd with "many other words." He solemnly and earnestly exhorted and encouraged them with words of comfort and hope. He persuaded, begged, besought, entreated, and implored them. And what was his solemn warning and hearts cry? *"Be saved from this crooked generation" (Acts 2:40).* Be delivered from this perverse age. Come out of this wicked way and come into a new way of wholeness and peace. A crooked generation is like a warped board that carpenters throw out because it is useless. It is twisted and perverse, turned away from the truth. It is a generation *"which has gone astray,"* according to the *New American Bible*.[9] Do all things without murmuring and disputing, that you may become blameless and harmless, children of God without fault in the midst of a crooked and perverse generation, among whom you shine as lights in the world *(Phil. 2:14–15)*. Repenting and turning to the Lord for salvation, being baptized in water and receiving the Holy Spirit, saves Christians from a crooked generation and leads them into a whole new way of life — the normal, overcoming, Christian life. Life and light is theirs. Full salvation was the message of the New Testament church.

> *Nor is there salvation in any other, for there is no other name under heaven given among men by which we must be saved.*
>
> *(Acts 4:12; see also 15:11)*

> *And he brought them out and said, "Sirs, what must I do to be saved?" So they said, "Believe on the Lord Jesus Christ, and you will be saved, you and your household."*   *(Acts 16:30–31)*

A NORMAL CHRISTIAN LIFE

Repentance, water baptism, and the gift of the Holy Spirit form the foundation for individual Christian lives as well as the foundation for the church.

Many Christians in the twentieth century think of salvation primarily in terms of heaven and hell. Their primary purpose for becoming a Christian is to escape hell. That is a good reason to be reconciled to God, but that is not the only reason Christ saves people. Peter's "many other words" did not deal with heaven or hell. They dealt with overcoming the present evil generation. Stressing the beginning of the journey and not the journey itself gives Christians a wrong focus and emphasis.

As Peter spoke, Rome was rapidly declining. The Jews had lived under the oppressive rule of Rome for 100 years. Immorality and darkness surrounded them. Now God was telling them how to overcome that evil generation and avoid the judgment that was surely coming upon them.

Believers today also need to overcome while living in the midst of an evil generation. They need to avoid being deceived by the present age. Tens of thousands of backsliders in the world today have not been able to live according to Peter's "many other words" and have fallen back into deception and sin.

Believers in the first church stood on a foundation of repentance. They validated their faith by obeying Christ's command to be baptized in water. They received the gift of the Holy Spirit. As a result, they enjoyed salvation and eternal life. They did not have an experiential or doctrinal separation between the elements of this foundation in their thinking. They accepted the foundation simply and completely. A properly laid foundation leads everyone to experience these things.

The twentieth-century church has been weakened by the separation of these foundational elements. "Do I have to be baptized in order to go to heaven?" "Do I have to be filled with the Holy Spirit?" It can all be yours, the entire New Covenant package! Why settle for anything less? ✠

STUDY QUESTIONS

1. In building according to God's pattern, how important is the foundation?

2. What is the first element in the foundation? What does it mean?

3. What is Charles Finney's definition of repentance?

4. List common misconceptions of repentance.

5. What is repentance based on?

6. What is the first sign of a convert's repentance?

7. What is it a sign of?

8. What is the baptism in the Holy Spirit?

9. What is a normal Christian life?

10. What were Peter's "many other words"?

3   *Added To the Church*

Then those who gladly received his word
were baptized: and that day about three
thousand souls were added to them. — Acts 2:41

N O ONE KNOWS HOW MANY PEOPLE HEARD PETER'S
Pentecost sermon. Perhaps tens of thousands. He called the
entire throng to repentance, asking for individual responses.
Some mocked and walked away. Others felt convicted but failed to
respond. The Bible says many were moved to make decisions and
take immediate action. Their repentance and faith were active —
not passive — and led to conviction, commitment, and immediate
change in their lives. No aspect of their lives was ever the same again.

BORN INTO THE KINGDOM

Those who actively responded to Peter's word showed great joy and
excitement. Acts reports they "gladly received" the message. Only
Luke among all New Testament writers uses this expression, and he
chose it only five other times. It means to receive kindly or heartily,
to welcome, embrace, or to accept with satisfaction. In classical
Greek it referred to accepting a teacher or his arguments.

The Holy Spirit anointed Peter's words, which convinced some
in the gathering to embrace the Gospel wholeheartedly. The ones
who repented experienced a transformation. Their baptism in water

gave outward proof that their inner man had been touched. Their baptism also gave them a new identity. Saved from their corrupt generation, they became members of a new community: the church.

Weymouth translates *v. 41* as: *"Those, therefore, who joyfully welcomed his Message were baptized."*[10] The *Jerusalem Bible* chooses these words: *"They were convinced by his arguments, and they accepted what he said and were baptized."*[11]

When a convert enters covenant relationship with Jesus he automatically chooses to identify with Christ's body, His bride, His church.

> *For by one Spirit we were all baptized into one body — whether Jews or Greeks, whether slaves or free — and have all been made to drink into one Spirit.* (1 Cor. 12:13)

The Scriptures declare that a person is born into the kingdom. Citizenship in the kingdom of God does not require ID or voting cards. Becoming a member of God's kingdom involves a radical change in identity and in lifestyle. All of a man's loyalties change simply because he has a new King. He is under new management and has received new marching orders.

> *Most assuredly, I say to you, unless one is born again, he cannot see the kingdom of God. ... Most assuredly, I say to you, unless one is born of water and the Spirit, he cannot enter the kingdom of God. That which is born of the flesh is flesh, and that which is born of me Spirit is spirit. Do not marvel that I said to you, "You must be born again."* (John 3:3, 5–7)

> *Since you have purified your souls in obeying the truth through the Spirit in sincere love of the brethren, love one another fervently*

with a pure heart, having been born again, not of corruptible
seed but incorruptible, through the word of God which lives and
abides forever.   *(1 Pet. 1:22–23)*

Whoever believes that Jesus is the Christ is born of God, and
everyone who loves Him who begot also loves him who is begotten
of Him. ... For whatever is born of God overcomes the world. And
this is the victory that has overcome the world — our faith.
                                    (1 John 5:1, 4; see also 3:9; 4:7)

JESUS STARTED HIS CHURCH

Near the end of His earthly ministry, Jesus introduced the word
church and used it twice. First, He referred to the *universal* church
that contains all believers from all times and all places. Second, He
referred to a specific, *local* church.

The first time, Jesus asked the disciples how they viewed Him.
"Who do you say that I am?" He inquired. Peter responded correctly,
"You are the Christ, the Son of the living God" *(Matt. 16:16)*. At that
point, Jesus taught them that He wanted to do more than reveal
Himself as the Messiah, the Son of God revealed in the flesh. He said
He had come to inaugurate a New Covenant community, which He
described as His church.

I will build My church, and the gates of Hades shall not prevail
against it.   *(Matt. 16:18)*

This reference speaks of the universal church.

The second time Jesus used the word church, He was coun-
seling the disciples on forgiveness. Problems in human relationships
create the need for forgiveness. Such a practical issue required practical instruction. Christ wanted members of His new community to

demonstrate committed love relationships including the desire to forgive each other. He instructed them:

> *Moreover if your brother sins against you, go and tell him his fault between you and him alone. If he hears you, you have gained your brother. But if he will not hear, take with you one or two more, that "by the mouth of two or three witnesses every word may be established." And if he refuses to hear them, tell it to the church. But if he refuses even to hear the church, let him be to you like a heathen and a tax collector.* (Matt. 18:15–17)

This second statement refers to a local group of committed believers, who gather for specific reasons at scheduled times. The local church is a visible community of no less than two or three believers with Jesus in their midst. It gathers in the name of the Lord and is linked to heaven. Each local church is the instrument of the kingdom of God in its own specific, geographic area. Christ gave authority to the local church to deal with offenses within the community.

> *Assuredly, I say to you, whatever you bind on earth will be bound in heaven, and whatever you loose on earth will be loosed in heaven. Again I say to you that if two of you agree on earth concerning anything that they ask, it will be done for them by My Father in heaven. For where two or three are gathered together in My name, I am there in the midst of them.* (Matt. 18:18–20)

People in Jerusalem who responded to Peter's preaching were born into the kingdom as they repented and were baptized. They automatically became members of the universal church, but that did not end the story. The Holy Spirit also began to form them into a visible, local church.

ADDING BELIEVERS

Many Christians today oppose any kind of official membership in the church. Some feel membership has the tendency to take the place of true conversion, so they throw out identification with the church. They look down on membership as if it were carnal — or even evil.

For nearly twenty years I pastored a church that was almost proud of the fact that it had nothing to join. The church was a fellowship without a membership. People would come when they wanted to. They would go when they wanted to. We had nothing to identify with. Yet *Acts 2:47* emphasizes the fact that the first believers were "added to the church." The first Christians definitely had a commitment to the pattern church in Jerusalem.

> *The idea of being added to the church is mentioned repeatedly as the church experienced dynamic growth. And that day about three thousand souls were added to them.* (Acts 2:41)

> *And believers were increasingly added to the Lord, multitudes of both men and women.* (Acts 5:14)

> *For he was a good man, full of the Holy Spirit and of faith. And a great many people were added to the Lord.* (Acts 11:24)

The word *added* means, to join, to become a part, to belong, or to be committed. It also means to put near, or to lay beside. In the Greek translation of the Old Testament, this word was used to refer to a proselyte who is joined to Israel.

Jesus used the word when He said, *"Seek the kingdom of God, and all these things shall be added to you"* (Luke 12:31). The disciples used the same word when they asked Jesus to *"increase [add to] our faith"* (Luke 17:5).

The verb in the passive voice indicates that the Holy Spirit took the initiative to add as new believers responded to the Spirit. Large numbers of souls added to the church brought a fulfillment to the following verse:

Your people shall be volunteers in the day of Your power; in the beauties of holiness, from the womb of the morning, you have the dew of Your youth. (Ps. 110:3)

After coming to Jesus Christ, some converts fall by the wayside because they do not see the importance of identifying with a local church. They think to themselves, "I identified with Jesus and that is enough." But when Christ started His church, it was not designed as an option for believers.

The church did not start with a go-it-alone, individualistic program. If it had, then *Acts*, chapter 2, would have said something like the following:

On the Day of Pentecost there was a great outpouring of the Spirit. Jesus was present, launched his church, and set it in order by heaven's design. The house of the Lord was established. Peter and the apostles held a great service where 3,000 new believers were baptized. As the sun went down, the crowd began to disperse. People departed for their homes. They were all excited about the wonderful day they had experienced. One of the new converts come up to Peter, shook his hand and said, "Thanks a lot, Peter, it was a wonderful day. I hope someday I will meet you again." And Peter said, "Yes, maybe I will see you again, Lord willing." And thus the great early church was launched!

The first Christians had come from several different nations, yet they did not all return to their home countries right away. They stayed in Jerusalem and identified with the first church. They sat under the apostles' teaching and grew in grace and knowledge.

CHRISTIAN VAGABONDS

A believer who never identifies with a local church wanders in a spiritual wilderness alone.

> *Like a bird that wanders from its nest is a man who wanders from his place.*　　　　　　　　　　　　　　　　　　*(Prov. 27:8)*

Adam's original sin caused a break in relationship with God and led to further isolation for Adam and his family. After Cain murdered his brother, he was cursed to wander as a vagabond in Nod.

> *'When you till the ground, it shall no longer yield its strength to you. A fugitive and a vagabond you shall be on the earth.' ... Then Cain went out from the presence of the Lord and dwelt in the land of Nod on the east of Eden.*　　　　　　　　　*(Gen. 4:12, 16)*

Nod means wanderer.

The nation of Israel under Moses had the same problem. The twelve tribes wandered in the wilderness with no place of their own.

> *They wandered in the wilderness in a desolate way; they found no city to dwell in. Hungry and thirsty, their soul fainted in them.*
> 　　　　　　　　　　　　　　　　　　　　　　*(Ps. 107:4–5)*

Some people think wandering around is exciting. The word *wander* means to be aimless, to have no purpose, to flee, stagger, to be depressed.

Later, Israel confessed they had sinned by wandering.

Our backslidings are many; we have sinned against you. (Jer. 14:7)

They refused to change their ways, so the Lord answered:

Thus says the Lord to this people: "Thus they have loved to wander; they have not restrained their feet. Therefore the Lord does not accept them; he will remember their iniquity now, and punish their sins." Then the Lord said to me, "Do not pray for this people, for their good. When they fast, I will not hear their cry; and when they offer burnt offering and grain offering, I will not accept them. But I will consume them by the sword, by the famine, and by the pestilence." (Jer. 14:10–12)

What a challenge that Scripture is to those who feel they do not need to be planted in a local church. Sad to say, many have simply never been taught that when they are saved they need to identify with a local, visible expression of the body of Christ. Like a newborn child, a new believer has a life of his own, but he cannot be separated from his parents. God plans for him to be set into a family.

God sets the solitary in families; he brings out those who are bound into prosperity; but the rebellious dwell in a dry land. (Ps. 68:6)

MEMBERS OF A BODY

The New Testament compares the church to a body. It is called the body of Christ.

And He [Christ] is the head of the body, the church.
(Col. 1:18; see also 2:19)

And He put all things under His [Christ's] feet, and gave Him to be head over all things to the church, which is His body.
(Eph. 1:22–23; see also 4:4).

For we, being many, are one bread and one body.   *(1 Cor. 10:17)*

Healthy, normal bodies have arms, legs, eyes, hands, and other distinctive parts. All the parts do unique jobs that serve the best interests of the whole body. They do not operate independently. They stay connected to each other.

For in fact the body is not one member but many.   *(1 Cor. 12:14)*

We have many members in one body, but all the members do not have the same function, so we, being many, are one body in Christ, and individually members of one another.   *(Rom. 12:4–5)*

For as the body is one and has many members, but all the members of that one body, being many, are one body, so also is Christ.
(1 Cor. 12:12)

Every believer needs the body of Christ. Everyone has a gift to contribute, and everyone needs the grace God ministers through others' gifts. Every member of the body is necessary and must be linked with others to function normally.

Arguments had crippled life and ministry in the Corinthian church. Division had stirred up turmoil. Like a human body, a church cannot function normally in disunity. Unity keeps a church running smoothly. The apostle Paul pleaded with church members to "speak the same thing, and that there be no divisions among you, but that you be perfectly joined together in the same mind and in the same judgment" *(1 Cor. 1:10).*

This appeal was not addressed to the universal church. It was addressed directly to members of a local church who failed to understand the importance of being added to one another. To illustrate every believer's need for the body of Christ, Paul compared spiritual gifts to parts of the body like feet, hands, eyes and ears.

> *If the foot should say, "Because I am not a hand, I am not of the body," is it therefore not of the body? And if the ear should say, "Because I am not an eye, I am not of the body," is it therefore not of the body? If the whole body were an eye, where would be the hearing? If the whole were hearing, where would be the smelling?*
> *(1 Cor. 12:15–17)*

Gifts are distributed throughout the body. No one has all the ministries and operations of the Spirit functioning in his life. Some Christians may think they have all nine gifts of the Spirit and need no one else, but that is completely contrary to the spirit of this text. No one can minister alone. A person may have a wonderful hand ministry, foot ministry, or ear ministry, but unless he is clearly and specifically related to the rest of the body he cannot fulfill his function. The work of the kingdom of God cannot be accomplished without the local church. All of the gifts and operations of the Spirit find their proper expression in the local church setting. No wonder the early believers immediately joined themselves to the church.

Paul also explained the gifts were given to benefit the whole body.

> *But the manifestation of the Spirit is given to each one for the profit of all.*   *(1 Cor. 12:7)*

Grace — not a person's merit — determines how gifts are given. Therefore, the gifted person has no reason for pride.

One and the same Spirit works all these things, distributing to each one individually as He wills. *(1 Cor. 12:11)*

God has set the members, each one of them, in the body just as He pleased. *(1 Cor. 12:18)*

God sets into the body everyone who has been born into the kingdom. Verse *18* (above) does not refer to membership in the universal church body. It refers to the local church body and the importance of every local member. It is God's will that everyone be set into a specific local church. This is not just Paul's idea. This is the Word of the Head of the church.

If anyone thinks himself to be a prophet or spiritual, let him acknowledge that the things which I write to you are the commandments of the Lord. *(1 Cor. 14:37)*

The message of the local church is one of the most important emphases of the Holy Spirit today. The Holy Spirit works in and through this chosen channel.

What if there were only one part to the body? What if everyone had exactly the same function? Then the body as a whole would not function. But God did not design the body that way. The body has many parts, and each one is necessary.

I do not "wine and dine" people to get them to come to church. I do not offer them jobs to guarantee their membership. The Lord's servants should strive always to be friendly and courteous to receive people with open arms, but not everyone who walks through the door is set here by God. A lot of people visit. It is God who sets every member into the body. My special interest is in those who are set here by the Lord.

SELFISH INDIVIDUALISM

Selfish individualism is the greatest weakness of the modern-day church. It is the primary obstacle to meaningful membership. Too many believers are satisfied that they simply are going to heaven instead of hell. They suffer from the Jesus-and-me syndrome. But that is not the biblical mandate.

Western culture focuses on individual identity, individual rights, etc. The 1990s have taken secular humanism to its logical conclusion. Every person is looking for himself, trying to find his identity. A fully autonomous individual is the goal of modem psychology. As a result, society is characterized by the absence of a sense of community. No one thinks about his corporate identity these days. Defining a person in terms of a group — even if it is the body of Christ — is cultural heresy. Covenant relationships have disappeared.

MEMBERSHIP IN THE CHURCH

Christians need to revive their identification with the body of Christ. It is one of the most foundational truths in the New Testament. To see it fulfilled, God must remove the "Lone Ranger" thinking from His people so He can place them into local churches where His varied gifts can function.

The Bible provides the following guidance on local church membership:[12]

1. Membership is implied by the tally of believers recorded in the New Testament. *Acts 2:41; 6:7.*

2. Membership is implied in the gathering together of specific groups. *1 Cor. 14:23; Acts. 14:27; 20:7; Heb. 10:25.*

3. Membership requires fulfillment of certain conditions; there-

fore, it is exclusive. Circumcision was required for members of the Old Testament congregation. The New Testament congregation requires a right relationship with Jesus Christ through repentance *(Matt. 3:2)*, humility and sacrifice *(Matt. 19:14–24)*, faith *(Mark 1:14–15)*, the new birth *(John 3:1–5)*, obedience *(Matt. 7:21)*, and endurance *(Luke 9:62)*. However, church attendance is open even to unbelievers *(James 2:2–4)*.

4. Membership is not to be seen as a matter of choice. Rejecting those whom Christ has sent, is the same as rejecting Christ *(Matt. 10:40; John 15:20)*. Refusing to join the church is like refusing to join oneself to Christ.

5. Membership should be recorded. No one could take proper care of God's sheep if no one knew who they were or where they belonged. It would make the job virtually impossible.

6. Membership should be transferred. The New Testament church used a letter of commendation *(Acts 18:27; Rom. 16:1; Col. 4:10; 2 Cor. 3:1–2)*.

THE PLANTING OF THE LORD

God is attempting to help His saints mature and become fruitful. This can take place only when they understand the importance of being added to the church. It is not enough just to say, "I'm a Christian." God wants believers to produce fruit, and fruit grows on trees that are planted.

This was the key to the ministry of Jesus. Quoting *Isaiah*, chapter *61*, He talked about the Spirit of the Lord being upon Him and that He was anointed to preach good tidings to the meek, to minister to the blind and the brokenhearted, to proclaim liberty to the captives, to open the prison for those that were bound. He went on to describe His ministry this way:

> *To console those who mourn in Zion, to give them beauty for ashes, the oil of joy for mourning, the garment of praise for the spirit of heaviness, that they might be called trees of righteousness, the planting of the Lord, that He may be glorified.* (Isa. 61:3)

To be added to the church is to be planted by the Lord in His house. Trees are planted to grow and produce fruit. Christians cannot be fruitful unless they have been planted in a place where they can put roots down, grow, and produce fruit.

A tumbleweed blowing through the desert might look impressive as it gathers other sticks, but it never produces fruit. A believer who refuses to allow himself to be planted in a local church is a spiritual tumbleweed. Looking for fruit on tumbleweeds leaves people sadly disappointed. That is why the Lord's ordained plan and pattern for every believer's life includes being planted.

> *The righteous shall flourish like a palm tree, he shall grow like a cedar in Lebanon. Those who are planted in the house of the Lord shall flourish in the courts of our God. They shall still bear fruit in old age; they shall be fresh and flourishing.* (Ps. 92:12–14)

Even people in a mobile ministry must have some place for their roots to go down. Paul consistently returned to Antioch to report to the brothers who were elders in the church there.

> *From there they sailed to Antioch, where they had been commended to the grace of God for the work which they had completed. Now when they had come and gathered the church together,*

they reported all that God had done with them, and that He had opened the door of faith to the Gentiles. So they stayed there a long time with the disciples. (Acts 14:26–28)

And when he had landed at Caesarea, and gone up and greeted the church, he went down to Antioch. (Acts 18:22)

The Scriptures refer not only to the necessity of planting but also to the need to be planted by a river.

Blessed is the man who walks not in the counsel of the ungodly, nor stands in the path of sinners, nor sits in the seat of the scornful; But his delight is in the law of the Lord, and in His law he meditates day and night. He shall be like a tree planted by the rivers of water, that brings forth its fruit in its season, whose leaf also shall not wither; and whatever he does shall prosper.

(Ps. 1:1–3; also see Jer. 17:7–8)

There is a river whose streams shall make glad the city of God, the holy place of the tabernacle of the Most High. God is in the midst of her, she shall not be moved; God shall help her, just at the break of dawn. (Ps. 46:4–5)

The river of God symbolizes life. It flows through the midst of the city and the tabernacle of God, both of which symbolize the church, the modern-day house of the Lord. To draw strength from the river, Christians must be planted like trees on the riverbank.

The local church gives believers a base to practice and polish their gifts. And before being exported, spiritual gifts must prove themselves at home. There must be a base from which to minister.

A young man carrying a trumpet came into my office one day. He said, "I am so frustrated. I have a real gift, but I don't have any outlet for it." He took the trumpet out of its case and began to play. He was talented. He could really blow that trumpet. Then with disgust he threw the trumpet onto the chair beside him and said, "No one will give me a place. I am so frustrated in my Christian walk."

I asked him a simple question, "Where is your home church?" He said he did not belong to any church. He explained that because he had this wonderful gift, he felt he should go from church to church and play his horn. His problem was his refusal to be planted. Because his roots were not in a river, he was not fulfilled in his gift.

Gifted believers should not refuse to minister in other churches. Many mobile ministries can prophesy and move mountains with their faith, but if they have not been planted in a specific local church, if their roots are not firmly placed in the river of God, in the city of God, eventually they will find themselves frustrated, barren and alone.

KINGDOM GROWTH

Being added to or planted in the house of God is of primary importance. It is no wonder Satan has perverted it and caused so much confusion over church membership. Without being added to the church, a believer will not find his place in the body or be fulfilled in his gift. Therefore, he will be subject to deception.

New Christians can be taught and brought to spiritual maturity when they find their places in the house of God and are planted members of that house.

Believers today who read their Bibles know 3,000 souls were added to the church on the Day of Pentecost. They know that fact only because early church leaders evidently took time to count the converts and keep track of them afterward. One hundred and twenty grew to 3,120. Much fruit was borne by the New Testament church. The foundation was built according to the pattern, and church membership grew tremendously.

Because the first believers were so responsive to the visitation of the Holy Spirit on Pentecost, they were very careful to build the first church exactly the way Jesus wanted them to. ✠

STUDY QUESTIONS

1. What was the evidence of true repentance among the new believers after the Day of Pentecost?

2. What does it mean to be born into the kingdom?

3. What are the two ways Jesus used the word church?

4. How does the local church relate to the kingdom of God?

5. What does it mean to be added to the church?

6. Why is local church membership important?

7. How does this relate to the revelation of the church as the body of Christ?

8. How does an individual believer become identified with a local church?

9. How does being added to the church relate to individual fruitfulness?

10. How does being added to the church relate to corporate fruitfulness?

4   *An Apostolic Team*

*And they continued steadfastly in the
apostles' doctrine ... many wonders and signs
were done through the apostles.*   — *Acts 2:42–43*

A T FIRST, THE TWELVE APOSTLES, INCLUDING MATTHIAS,
governed the Jerusalem congregation of 3,000 to 8,000 members. As the church grew, the Lord provided more gifted leaders
and formed them into powerful instruments of His authority. The
leadership team was well-structured and effective.

All authority belongs to the Lord, but people have questioned
God's authority and rebelled against it ever since the Serpent told
Eve she could be like God. Self-centeredness lies at the heart of
sin, and the first manifestation of sin is rebellion. Man was tempted
to launch out on his own rather than trust God's authority. He fell
when he declared his independence from God. People have been in
trouble ever since.

Jesus said, "All authority has been given to Me in heaven and
on earth" *(Matt. 28:18)*. However, the Lord chose to work together
with human beings. He delegates some of His authority to human
instruments *(see Rom. 13:1–4)*. Authority establishes boundaries for
human behavior. Ironically, people find freedom and creativity
within boundaries.

Rebellion is resistance to authority. Since God is behind all delegated authority, rebellion resists God. People do not want anyone else telling them what to do. They invent philosophies, theologies, and policies to justify their rebellion. So many issues in the church and in believers' personal lives come down to a question of authority.

Another word for rebellion is lawlessness. It refers to life without restraints, laws, or rules. Without divine authority, lawlessness prevails.

In those days there was no king in Israel; everyone did what was
right in his own eyes. (Judg. 17:6; see also 21:25)

For just as you presented your members as slaves of uncleanness,
and of lawlessness leading to more lawlessness, so now present
your members as slaves of righteousness for holiness.
(Rom. 6:19; see also 2 Thess. 2:7)

... those who walk according to the flesh in the lust of uncleanness
and despise authority. They are presumptuous, self-willed. They
are not afraid to speak evil of dignitaries. (2 Pet. 2:10)

Whoever commits sin also commits lawlessness,
and sin is lawlessness. (1 John 3:4)

The New Testament church had elders and a clear pattern of authority.[13] Some elders were ordained to govern the house of God. But for authority to operate, believers had to respond submissively by sacrificing their pride and rebellion.

Likewise you younger people, submit yourselves to your elders.
Yes, all of you be submissive to one another, and be clothed with
humility, for "God resists the proud, but gives grace to the humble."
(1 Pet. 5:5)

Remember those who rule over you, who have spoken the word of God to you, whose faith follow, considering the outcome of their conduct. (Heb. 13:7)

Obey those who rule over you, and be submissive, for they watch out for your souls, as those who must give account. Let them do so with joy and not with grief, for that would be unprofitable for you. (Heb. 13:17)

Every Christian needs to settle the authority issue in his own heart so he can freely study the subject.

AUTHORITY IN THE OLD TESTAMENT

Authority requires a structure or organization. For authority to be effective, it must be channeled in a disciplined way.

Where there is no counsel, the people fall; but in the multitude of counselors there is safety. (Prov. 11:14; see also 15:22; 24:6)

The Bible shows patterns of divine authority, for the family, society, and the house of God.

The Family The first family involved two parents, Adam and Eve. The Lord created Eve as a suitable helper for Adam in the work in the Garden of Eden. She was made equivalent to him to complement him in governing creation. Together they had authority over the children the Lord gave them. The family formed the foundation for authority in society.

Jethro's Principle Out of Egypt, Moses led a community of more than 600,000 men plus their wives and children. As time passed, the work of governing proved too much for him. His father-in-law, Jethro, visited Israel's camp. Jethro saw that even though Moses wore himself out ministering to people, some legitimate needs were not met.

He advised Moses to share his responsibilities with other qualified leaders. Moses implemented Jethro's advice, which mirrors God's pattern of authority (or it would not be recorded in *Exod. 18:19–23*).

Moses appointed men qualified by righteous character to work with him on a leadership team. Some leaders had grace to oversee large groups and some worked with small groups. They were structured according to the number of people they served: 10, 50, 100 or 1,000. Moses took ongoing responsibility for prayer, for representing the people before God, and for teaching the Word and ways of the Lord to the people. The nation followed this pattern, and later the church adopted it.

Elders of Israel   Most ancient societies had elders whose maturity and wisdom qualified them to lead their tribes. (For examples see *Gen. 50:7; Num. 22:4, 7*.) Israel also had tribal elders who led their respective tribes and their nation as a whole. (For examples see *Exod. 3:16, 18; 4:29; 12:21; 17:5, 6; 18:12; 19:7; 24:1, 9, 14; Lev. 4:15; 9:1; Deut. 5:23; 27:1; 31:9, 28; 32:7*.) When Israel settled permanently in the Promised Land, elders ruled the cities. (See *Deut. 19:12; 21:2, 3, 4, 6, 19, 20; 22:15–18; 25:7–9; 29:10*.)

Moses called on Israel's tribal elders to help him govern. Burdened by the weight of leading so many people, he needed their help. The Lord told him to choose seventy elders to form a leadership council. Then the Lord anointed the elders to help shoulder the load of leadership for the nation.

> *"I am not able to bear all these people alone, because the burden is too heavy for me. If You treat me like this, please kill me here and now — if I have found favor in Your sight — and do not let me see my wretchedness!" So the LORD said to Moses: "Gather to Me seventy men of the elders of Israel, whom you know to be the elders of the people and officers over them; bring them to the tabernacle of meeting, that they may stand there with you. Then I will come down and talk with you there. I will take of the Spirit that is upon*

you and will put the same upon them; and they shall bear the burden of the people with you, that you may not bear it yourself alone."   *(Num. 11:14–17; see also 11:24–25, 30; 16:25)*

Priests and Levites   Spiritual leadership in the house of God was given to Aaron and his sons. As priests, they interceded for the people before God and lead the congregation in worship. However, the work of the ministry was too great for Aaron's family, so men from the tribe of Levi were assigned to help as assistant priests. The Lord took the Levites as substitutes for the firstborn of every family.

And you shall stand the Levites before Aaron and his sons, and then offer them like a wave offering to the Lord. Thus you shall separate the Levites from among the children of Israel, and the Levites shall be Mine. After that the Levites shall go in to service the tabernacle of meeting. So you shall cleanse them and offer them, like a wave offering. For they are wholly given to Me from among the children of Israel; I have taken them for Myself instead of all who open the womb, the firstborn of all the children of Israel. And I have given the Levites as a gift to Aaron and his sons from among the children of Israel, to do the work for the children of Israel in the tabernacle of meeting, and to make atonement for the children of Israel, that there be no plague among the children of Israel when the children of Israel come near the sanctuary.

(Num. 8:13–16, 19)

AUTHORITY IN THE NEW TESTAMENT

Elders governed the first church. They gave themselves to care for, pastor, or shepherd the people. Their godly character qualified them to lead, and they held the office of overseer.

Elders — The Character   The word translated elder is the Greek *presbúteros*. It means senior or older, in contrast to a novice. It describes a man's character quality, not his office or position of authority. Since the nature of the church is spiritual, an elder can be spiritually mature without being aged. "For by it the elders obtained a good testimony" *(Heb. 11:2; see also Rev. 4:4, 10; 5:5, 6, 8, 11, 14; 7:11, 13; 11:16; 14:3; 19:4)*. Eventually, the word elder came to designate an official position of authority.

> *When they had appointed elders in every church, and prayed with fasting, they commended them to the Lord in whom they had believed.* (Acts 14:23)

> *They also ... sent it to the elders by the hands of Barnabas and Saul.* (Acts 11:30)

At first, apostles governed the church. Later, apostles and elders governed it.

> *They determined that Paul and Barnabas and certain others of them should go up to Jerusalem, to the apostles and elders, about this question.* (Acts 15:2; see also 15:4, 6, 22, 23; 16:4)

The apostles were considered elders.

The elders who are among you I exhort, I who am a fellow elder.
(1 Pet. 5:1)

Eventually elders were appointed in all local churches and honored for upholding responsibility.

For this reason I left you in Crete, that you should set in order the things that are lacking, and appoint elders in every city as I commanded you. *(Titus 1:5)*

Let the elders who rule well be counted worthy of double honor.
(1 Tim. 5:17)

Elders lead by example. They qualify to lead others because of their character, moral life, and personal relationship with the Lord, not because of their charisma or ability. Character develops over time and is proven. Paul outlined specific character qualifications for elders who oversee congregations:

For this reason I left you in Crete, that you should set in order the things that are lacking, and appoint elders in every city as I commanded you — if a man is blameless, the husband of one wife, having faithful children not accused of dissipation or insubordination. For a bishop must be blameless, as a steward of God, not self-willed, not quick-tempered, not given to wine, not violent, not greedy for money, but hospitable, a lover of what is good, sober-minded, just, holy, self-controlled, holding fast the faithful word as he has been taught, that he may be able, by sound doctrine, both to exhort and convict those who contradict. *(Titus 1:5–9)*

A bishop then must be blameless, the husband of one wife, temperate, sober-minded, of good behavior, hospitable, able to teach; not given to wine, not violent, not greedy for money, but gentle, not quarrelsome, not covetous; one who rules his own house well, having his children in submission with all reverence (for if a man does not know how to rule his own house, how will he take care of the church of God?); not a novice, lest being puffed up with pride he fall into the same condemnation as the devil. Moreover he must have a good testimony among those who are outside, lest he fall into reproach and the snare of the devil. (1 Tim. 3:2–7)

Overseer — The Office   Paul told Titus to appoint elders but listed qualifications for the office of an *overseer* or *bishop*. The Greek word translated overseer is *epískopoi*. Gentiles understood *epískopoi*, so Paul, the apostle to the Gentiles, used it. Among Greeks, it referred to a commissioner appointed to rule a new colony. It is synonymous with elder and is used five times in the New Testament. It describes an office or position of authority and refers to the ordained elder who oversees church activity *(1 Tim. 4:14; Titus 1:5)*.

Pastor — The Work   The Greek noun *poimēn* describes the work of elders *(John 21:16; Acts 20:28; 1 Pet. 5:2)*. It is translated *shepherd* sixteen times and pastor one time. The verb *poimaínō* is translated *feed* or *tend* seven times and *rule* or *shepherd* four times. Four times it refers to Jesus *(Matt. 2:6; Rev. 7:17; 12:5; 19:15)*.

He said to him again a second time, "Simon, son of Jonah, do you love Me?" He said to Him, "Yes, Lord; You know that I love You." He said to him, "Tend My sheep." (John 21:16)

The work of the elder is pastoring or shepherding God's flock. He leads sheep into green pastures. He must passionately love the Word of God and have a solid personal relationship with Christ. The Bible exhorts elders to give themselves to study and meditation in the Word to prepare effective teaching and preaching to guide God's people.

Meditate on these things; give yourself entirely to them, that your progress may be evident to all. Take heed to yourself and to the doctrine. Continue in them, for in doing this you will save both yourself and those who hear you. (1 Tim. 4:15–16)

Let the elders who rule well be counted worthy of double honor, especially those who labor in the word and doctrine. (1 Tim. 5:17)

Preach the word! Be ready in season and out of season. Convince, rebuke, exhort, with all longsuffering and teaching. (2 Tim. 4:2)

Shepherds tend to the sheep's needs as God's representatives.

Is anyone among you sick? Let him call for the elders of the church, and let them pray over him, anointing him with oil in the name of the Lord. (James 5:14)

The words elder, overseer, and pastor touch three different aspects of the leadership function. It is a mistake to separate them because they overlap. The following passages contain all three terms and show how they interrelate:

From Miletus he sent to Ephesus and called for the elders of the church. Therefore take heed to yourselves and to all the flock, among which the Holy Spirit has made you overseers, to shepherd the church of God which He purchased with His own blood.
(Acts 20:17, 28)

The elders who are among you I exhort, I who am a fellow elder and a witness of the sufferings of Christ, and also a partaker of the glory that will be revealed: Shepherd the flock of God which is among you, serving as overseers, not by compulsion but willingly, not for dishonest gain but eagerly. (1 Pet. 5:1–2)

Deacons — The Assistants   Like Moses, early church elders found their work overwhelming. New converts brought needs with them. More people meant more needs. Elders needed a second tier of authority — another group of leaders — who would assist in the ministry. They turned to the pool of 120 disciples who had been in the upper room and had been trained by the Master Teacher for three and one-half years. Seven men were selected.

> *Now in those days, when the number of the disciples was multiplying, there arose a murmuring against the Hebrews by the Hellenists, because their widows were neglected in the daily distribution. Then the twelve summoned the multitude of the disciples and said, "It is not desirable that we should leave the word of God and serve tables. Therefore, brethren, seek out from among you seven men of good reputation, full of the Holy Spirit and wisdom, whom we may appoint over this business; but we will give ourselves continually to prayer and to the ministry of the word."*   (Acts 6:1–4)

The assistants were called deacons. The word deacon is derived from the Greek word *diákonos* which means minister or servant. It was used originally for an attendant or waiter, but took on greater meaning in the New Testament. This word is used thirty times in the New Testament. It is used of the office only in *Phil. 1:1* and *1 Tim. 3:8, 12.*

> *Paul and Timothy, bondservants of Jesus Christ, To all the saints in Christ Jesus who are in Philippi, with the bishops and deacons.*
> *(Phil. 1:1)*

With the help of deacons, "the word of God spread, and the number of the disciples multiplied greatly in Jerusalem, and a great many of the priests were obedient to the faith" *(Acts 1:7).*

Deacons assisted the Twelve in all aspects of ministry. Philip was the first evangelist, and Stephen was the first martyr of the church. They were anointed leaders, true men of God in their own right.

And Stephen, full of faith and power, did great wonders and signs among the people. (Acts 6:8)

Like elders, the deacons qualified by their exemplary character. Paul's list of qualifications for deacons looks almost identical to qualifications for elders, the chief difference being deacons were not required to be able to teach *(see 1 Tim. 3:8–13)*.

TEAM MINISTRY

Eldership was collegial in nature. It was team ministry. Men with individual powers and duties subordinated personal interests and opinions to pursue a common goal. As peers, all watched over the flock. A plural leadership spoke with one voice. It took joint action. Each person protected the unity and efficiency of the group. The only Scriptures where elder is singular is *1 Tim. 5:19; 1 Pet. 5:1* (speaking of Peter)*; 2 John 1 & 3 John 1* (speaking of John).

Western individualism makes it hard for Christians to be good church members and doubly hard to be good leaders. Personal ambition and aggression usually characterize leadership, but Jesus taught a different kind of leadership. He taught the revolutionary ideal of servant-leadership.

Jesus called them to Himself and said, "You know that the rulers of the Gentiles lord it over them, and those who are great exercise authority over them. Yet it shall not be so among you; but whoever desires to become great among you, let him be your servant. And whoever desires to be first among you, let him be your slave — just as the Son of Man did not come to be served, but to serve, and to give His life a ransom for many."   (Matt. 20:25–28)

To Jesus, more authority meant more opportunity to serve more people. To serve a large number of people, leadership has to be provided by a team of gifted leaders — a "multitude of counselors" (Prov. 11:14).

Here are some benefits of team ministry:[14]

1. It provides a total ministry. Working together, men with different ministries and roles produce a complete ministry that can properly care for the needs of the people.

2. It provides a variety of ministries. The ministers on a team have different personalities just as the people to whom they minister are different. Individuals relate to some ministers more than to others. Where a variety of shepherds tend the flock, sheep flourish best.

3. It accelerates productivity. More work can be accomplished by the labor of several people, coordinated and working together, than by the same number of people working alone or separately.

4. It confirms truth. A team of voices speaking the same thing establishes the truth of God in the hearts and lives of people more effectively than a single voice.

5. It encourages new ideas. An eldership team contains a variety of opinions, viewpoints, approaches and methods. Truth can bear inspection. Leaders can freely express their opinions and never break rank, never break the unity of the spirit, never break fellowship.

6. It provides checks and balances. Individual elders are accountable to one another and more likely to avoid the common pitfalls of leadership.

7. It assures smooth transitions. Sending out Paul and Barnabus did not stop the effectiveness of the elders' leadership.

8. It provides fulfillment. Each one must fulfill only the role he is uniquely gifted for. The church must rid itself of the mentality that ministers must perform solo. That concept has to be readjusted. Looking beyond the solo minister reveals — all of a sudden — leaders throughout the congregation who have strength and much to offer in their area of expertise, in their God-given role.

9. It facilitates growth. Doubling the number of elders in a growing church does not merely double the number of people the elders can handle. Instead, the number of people the elders can manage increases geometrically.

10. It preserves ministers. They are less likely to collapse under the load if they have a team to share the weight of it.

HEADSHIP: THE TEAM LEADER

Everywhere God delegates His authority, He appoints someone to be the head. It is true in the family. It is true in government. It is also true in the church. Every team needs a captain. Every organization requires someone to coordinate and represent the whole. Someone needs to have the representative responsibility for the group. The Bible refers to this as headship.

> But I want you to know that the head of every man is Christ, the head of woman is man, and the head of Christ is God. *(1 Cor. 11:3)*

> *For the husband is head of the wife, as also Christ is head of the church; and He is the Savior of the body.* (Eph. 5:23)

Every eldership team must have a head or senior elder. As the captain of the team he is a "first among equals" and is responsible to keep everything functioning smoothly and steadily. This role is vital to team ministry.

The presiding elder is a player-coach. Besides moving in his specific spiritual gift to edify the whole body, He serves the other team ministers by moderating, coordinating, encouraging, expediting, evaluating, alerting, and motivating. Not everyone can function as a senior elder. A specific gift-mix is required to coordinate the ministry of an entire team.

In Jesus' day, Jewish synagogues were governed by a council of elders. Each council of elders *gerousía* had a president *gerousiárchēs* who was appointed for life. He was also called the "ruler of the synagogue" *(Acts 18:8, 17)*.

The pattern of authority in the New Testament includes the role of head elder. *"And after they had become silent, James answered, saying, 'Men and brethren, listen to me'" (Acts 15:13)*. Apostles also functioned as senior elders *(Titus 1:5; 2 John 1)*.

Some deny the truth of headship authority in the church. Those people — usually men — believe in headship in the home but not in the church! How could headship apply to one area of delegated authority and not to another?[15]

God blesses team ministry. It accomplishes His purpose of ministry to the body and to the world by His Holy Spirit. Under team ministry, the early church prospered, spread rapidly, and turned the whole Roman world upside down.

FIVE LEADERSHIP GIFTS

An elder blends godly character with leadership gifts to serve the body. Christ wants a glorious church without spot or wrinkle *(Eph. 5:27)* and has provided five leadership gifts to help the church fulfill His plan.

> *And God has appointed these in the church: first apostles, second prophets, third teachers, after that miracles, then gifts of healings, helps, administrations, varieties of tongues.* *(1 Cor. 12:28)*

> *And He Himself gave some to be apostles, some prophets, some evangelists, and some pastors and teachers.* *(Eph. 4:11)*

No elder has enough ability, anointing, or grace to serve an entire congregation of saints the way the Lord wills. Since no one has all the gifts given by God, He puts together teams of leaders with a variety of gifts "for the equipping of the saints for the work of ministry, for the edifying of the body of Christ" *(Eph. 4:12)*.

These ministries were not given just for a particular age. They were given to function "until we all come to the unity of the faith" *(Eph. 4:13)*. They were given until the church achieves the "measure of the stature of the fullness of Christ." Apart from this God-given government, God's purpose never will be realized.

Christ did not provide gifted leaders to be professional doers of the work. They shepherd, train, and equip the saints who do the work of the ministry. And all the saints in the body are needed to finish the work.

Pastors The most familiar gift is the pastor. Pastors are given to rule over or shepherd local assemblies. The term pastor summarizes the work of the local elders. A true shepherd will:

1. Feed the sheep *(1 Pet. 5:2)*.

2. Guide, lead, and govern the sheep *(1 Pet. 5:2)*.
3. Love the souls of the sheep *(Heb. 13:17)*.
4. Care for the sheep *(John 10:13)*.
5. Lay down his life for the sheep *(John 10:15–18)*.
6. Defend the flock in times of trouble *(John 10:12)*.

Teachers   Along with pastors, teachers feed the Word of God to the flock. Feeding is the primary task of shepherding, and all elders are to be able to teach.

> *Now in the church that was at Antioch there were certain prophets and teachers.*   *(Acts 13:1)*

> *I was appointed a preacher and an apostle — I am speaking the truth in Christ and not lying — a teacher of the Gentiles in faith and truth.*   *(1 Tim. 2:7)*

The teaching ministry builds the edifice on the foundation of the local church. Teachers open the Bible and expose the Scriptures, giving the saints deep roots in the Word of God. They are essential to the perfecting of the saints. God has promised to restore true teachers to the church in these days.

> *And though the Lord gives you the bread of adversity and the water of affliction, yet your teachers will not be moved into a corner anymore, but your eyes shall see your teachers.*   *(Isa. 30:20)*

Teachers, apostles, and prophets are listed without pastors in *1 Cor. 12:28*. Some Bible commentators say the grammatical structure of *Eph. 4:11* blends the pastor and teacher into one rather than two separate gifts.

Evangelists   The best known gift next to pastors is the evangelist. The word evangelist describes one who proclaims good news. It is used only three times in the New Testament. Paul instructs Timothy to do the work of an evangelist *(2 Tim. 4:5)*. In this sense an evangelist is an assistant apostle in the work of church planting.

> *But you be watchful in all things, endure afflictions, do the work of an evangelist, fulfill your ministry.*   *(2 Tim. 4:5)*

The ministry of Philip pictures the work of an evangelist.

> *On the next day we who were Paul's companions departed and came to Caesarea, and entered the house of Philip the evangelist, who was one of the seven, and stayed with him*   *(Acts 21:8)*

Philip's ministry was two-dimensional. He preached publicly *(Acts 8:1–13)*, and witnessed one-on-one *(vv. 26–40)*. His ministry broke new ground with the Gospel and was accompanied by healing and miracle signs. In all his methods, he was obedient to the Spirit of God and was conscious of his own limitations. He certainly did not feel that he was self-sufficient. The final result of his work was the birth of a local church.

Prophets   Prophets were prominent in the first church. They have a two-dimensional gift to the body of Christ. Like the prophets of old, they have a ministry of foretelling and forthtelling. They foretell the future as God reveals it by His Spirit, and they speak or "bubble forth" a Word from God to their present generation.

> *Now Judas and Silas, themselves being prophets also, exhorted and strengthened the brethren with many words.*   *(Acts 15:32)*

> *... built on the foundation of the apostles and prophets, Jesus Christ*
> *Himself being the chief cornerstone.*   *(Eph. 2:20; see also 3:5)*

The prophet bears responsibility for having a prophetic view of present conditions. He also must be open to receiving a predictive word from God. He works most closely with the apostle, and both are foundational ministries *(Eph. 2:20)*. Agabus is the most notable prophet in the book of *Acts*. He foretold a famine and the imprisonment of Paul.

> *And in these days prophets came from Jerusalem to Antioch. Then*
> *one of them, named Agabus, stood up and showed by the Spirit*
> *that there was going to be a great famine throughout all the world,*
> *which also happened in the days of Claudius Caesar.*
> *(Acts 11:27–28; see also 21:10–14)*

Prophets minister in corporate assemblies to the body of Christ *(1 Cor. 14:29–37)*; in ordaining and sending out ministries under the auspices of the local assembly *(Acts 13:3)*; and in exhortation, edification and comfort to the whole body *(1 Cor. 14:3)*.

A prophet must:
1. Have the gift of prophecy *(1 Cor. 12:10)*.
2. Be appointed by God *(1 Cor. 12:28, 29)*.
3. Exhibit a life of holiness and humility.
4. Be willing to have his prophecies judged *(1 Cor. 14:29)*.

Apostles The Greek word *apóstolos* means one who is sent. The classical Greek use of *apostéllo* refers to an ambassador sent with a group of colonists to establish a new colony. An apostle was sent with authority to faithfully represent the purpose and intention of his sender.

Apostles are foundation builders *(Eph. 2:20)*. They coordinate local church planting *(1 Cor. 9:1–2)*. They are spiritual fathers of spiritual fathers. They are pastors of pastors. They may be called on to work with assemblies that are already established but need further grounding.

The word apostle is used eight times in the Gospels, thirty-three in Acts, forty in the epistles, and twice in Revelation. An examination of these passages leads to the following conclusions:

1. The twelve apostles were intimately involved with the Lord and were present at the foundation supper of the New Covenant *(Luke 22:14)*. They have a special place in the kingdom.

2. Other apostles ministered in the church, men like Andronicus *(Rom. 16:7)*, Barnabas, Paul *(Acts 14:14)*, Titus *(2 Cor. 8:23)*, Timothy *(1 Thess. 1:1; 2:6)* and others.

Not everyone believes that apostles continued to minister beyond the death of the Twelve. However, the job description for New Testament apostles applies to more than the work of the Twelve. In addition, the New Testament names more apostles than the Twelve, indicating that the gift functioned normally in local churches and was not limited to the Twelve.

The ministry of the apostle never was rescinded in the New Testament. *Rev. 21:14* refers to the "apostles of the Lamb." The original Twelve could not be replaced. However, the other apostles could be and were replaced.

Apostles require a mature age to lead a new generation of leaders. They may begin as pastors, evangelists, or teachers but develop apostolic authority as their ministry matures.

Accounts of the apostle John's life picture how New Testament apostles seem to function. John lived in Ephesus, the chief city of the Roman province of Asia. The "mother church" of that province was in Ephesus, and John had apostolic responsibility for all the churches and elders. He was "the elder" among an entire body of elders.

John had a problem with a leader in one of the churches under his authority. Diotrephes, evidently the chief elder of a local church, had rejected John's apostolic oversight. The reason: He "loves to be first" *(3 John 9)*. Diotrephes did not have the support of Gaius and other elders, who evidently called John for help.[16]

> *Therefore, if I come, I will call to mind his deeds which he does, prating against us with malicious words. And not content with that, he himself does not receive the brethren, and forbids those who wish to, putting them out of the church.*　　　　*(3 John 10)*

The elders of the church had come under John's apostolic authority voluntarily. When they called on him, he personally assisted them.

Qualifications of an apostle include:[17]
1. The heart of a father *(1 Cor. 4:15; Phil. 2:22)*,
2. A deep love for and loyalty to the church of God *(1 Cor. 13)*,
3. Patience *(2 Cor. 12:12)*,
4. Humility. He must not be given to self-glory *(1 Thess. 2:6; 1 Cor. 4:9; 2 Cor. 10:8)*,
5. A servant's heart *(Rom. 1:1; Phil. 1:1)*.

RESTORING SPIRITUAL AUTHORITY

The first church had mature, gifted, strong leaders. Elders and deacons provided clear authority structures in every local church. Each leadership team had a definite chief or captain. Each one also had a spiritual father who provided apostolic covering. God's delegated authority provided strength and safety for His people.

When the New Testament apostles all died, the church did not know how to replace them. Rather than ask the Lord to raise a new generation of spiritual fathers, the second-century church institutionalized itself. Each assembly took its chief elder, elevated him to a level of authority over other elders, and called him the bishop. The bishop of a mother church functioned as the archbishop or the bishop over other bishops in his region. Eventually the bishop of the church at Rome was considered to be the highest bishop of all.[18]

True New Testament authority is being restored. Pastors, teachers, and evangelists already have been restored. During the twentieth century, true prophets were restored. Now it is time to believe the Lord for the restoration of true apostles.

Older men of God need to pastor the younger generation of pastors. To function successfully, an eldership team needs an effective, local, chief elder and a mature, proven apostle outside the local church to call on when needed.

The church does not need more bureaucratic institutions. It needs true apostles restored to function with spiritual authority based on voluntary, personal relationships. Only then will the church grow to maturity.

We should no longer be children, tossed to and fro and carried about with every wind of doctrine, by the trickery of men, in the cunning craftiness of deceitful plotting, but, speaking the truth in love, may grow up in all things into Him who is the head — Christ.
(Eph. 4:14–15) ✠

STUDY QUESTIONS

1. What is rebellion?

2. Why is the presence of authority in the church important?

3. What is the first place authority is found?

4. What was the pattern of authority in Israel?

5. What was the pattern of authority in the New Testament church?

6. What qualifies someone to have authority in the church?

7. What is the work of a leader in the church?

8. Why is it important for those in authority in the church to lead together as a team?

9. What are the leadership gifts the Lord gives the church?

10. What is the role of an apostle in the church today?

5 An Apostolic Fellowship

And they continued steadfastly in the
apostles' doctrine and fellowship. — *Acts 2:42*

W ITH ZEAL 3,000 NEW BELIEVERS TURNED TOWARD
their new opportunity to live out their faith. The first Christians
hungered for the apostles' teaching, prayed with tenacity, and
worshipped wholeheartedly. They were not passive or neutral about
it. They "continued steadfastly" in their commitment to God and to
the apostolic fellowship. They had a passionate commitment.

Luke describes the believers' zeal with a Greek word that is fairly
rare in the New Testament. The word communicates an intense, con-
sistent dedication. It means to persist in adhering to something, to
be intently engaged, or to attend constantly. A verb in the imperfect tense, it signifies continuous action: "they kept on continuing
steadfastly" in day-to-day commitment. These believers possessed
wholehearted devotion.

Luke used this powerful word several other times. The 120 disciples who gathered in the upper room "*continued* with one accord
in prayer and supplication" *(Acts 1:14)*. The first church members
were "*continuing* daily with one accord in the temple" *(Acts 2:46)*. After
the congregation grew into a so-called "megachurch," the apostles
declared their intention to "give ourselves *continually* to prayer and
to the ministry of the word" *(Acts 6:4)*.

As a result of Peter's preaching, many present on the Day of Pentecost dedicated themselves to a whole new way of life. The *Amplified Bible* translates verse *42* as: *"And they steadfastly persevered, devoting themselves constantly to the instruction and fellowship of the apostles."*[19] Believers' lives were marked by: *(1)* the apostles' doctrine, *(2)* fellowship, *(3)* the breaking of bread, and *(4)* prayers.

PRIORITY OF DOCTRINE

First, the new congregation dedicated itself to the apostles' doctrine. Daily reading and teaching built strong foundations in believers' lives. They sought the Word of God for guidance and did not think it was optional. They found answers to their questions in the Scriptures. They did not rely only on their experience. All 3,120 members studied the ways of God.[20] No wonder they preached the Gospel with clarity to the whole world, beginning in Jerusalem, and gave reasons for the hope that was within them.

To enjoy the same experience today, Christians must believe that the Bible is God's inspired Word. It not only contains God's Word; it is God's Word. The very words and phrases of the Bible are inspired by God.

> *But you must continue in the things which you have learned and been assured of, knowing from whom you have learned them, and that from childhood you have known the Holy Scriptures, which are able to make you wise for salvation through faith which is in Christ Jesus. All Scripture is given by inspiration of God, and is profitable for doctrine, for reproof, for correction, for instruction in righteousness, that the man of God may be complete, thoroughly equipped for every good work.* (2 Tim. 3:14–17)

The word *inspired* means God-breathed. The Lord breathed out by His Spirit and gave specific, written revelation of Himself. This sacred writing is the only objective, authoritative revelation God has given and is the absolute truth of God.

Sanctify them by Your truth. Your word is truth.　　　*(John 17:17)*

Man's search for truth starts at the Word of God. Objective, absolute truth is found only in God's written Word. Man cannot begin with his own experience, interpret it to make sense to him, then search the Scripture for support of his interpretation. Instead he must interpret his experience in light of the Word. This pattern works for studies in philosophy, psychology, and theology.

More and more people in western culture do not believe absolute truth exists. They think every individual has the luxury of defining truth for himself. That would be true if God had not revealed truth in the Bible.

Principles found in the Bible build maturity and stability into Christ's disciples. They stand on the unchangeable Word of God and do not live by impulse. They have the only authoritative source of truth and principles for faith and morals.

Any church that accomplishes great things in the kingdom of God must have a firm foundation in the Scripture. Members must know the ways of God, the mind of God, and the eternal purpose of God. They must center ministries around biblical priorities — like the first church — and not around men's charisma.

Then Philip opened his mouth, and beginning at this Scripture, preached Jesus to him.　　　*(Acts 8:35)*

Then Paul, as his custom was, went in to them, and for three Sabbaths reasoned with them from the Scriptures.　　　*(Acts 17:2)*

Now a certain Jew named Apollos, born at Alexandria, an elo-
quent man and mighty in the Scriptures, came to Ephesus. ... for he
vigorously refuted the Jews publicly, showing from the Scriptures
that Jesus is the Christ. (Acts 18:24, 28)

Paul gave the Bereans a very high complement.

These were more fair-minded than those in Thessalonica, in that
they received the word with all readiness, and searched the Scrip-
tures daily to find out whether these things were so. (Acts 17:11)

The word *doctrine* in Greek is *didachē*. It refers to teaching,
instruction, or the subjects taught. In the Great Commission, the
Lord gave the church a mandate to teach. He instructed the apostles
to make disciples, "teaching them to observe all things that I have
commanded you" *(Matt. 28:19–20)*.

Luke refers to doctrine three other times. The Jewish Sanhedrin
condemned the apostles, telling them, "Look, you have filled
Jerusalem with your doctrine" *(Acts 5:28)*. On the island of Cyprus Paul
preached the Gospel to the Roman proconsul who was "astonished
at the teaching of the Lord" *(Acts 13:12)*. The Greek philosophers in
Athens requested of Paul, "May we know what this new doctrine is
of which you speak?" *(Acts 17:19)*.

The ministry of the apostles and the lives of the disciples revolved
around the preaching and teaching of the Word. Note the following:

However, many of those who heard the word believed. (Acts 4:4)

... and they were all filled with the Holy Spirit, and they spoke the
word of God with boldness. (Acts 4:31)

... but we will give ourselves continually to prayer and to the min-
istry of the word. (Acts 6:4)

Then the word of God spread, and the number of the disciples mul-
tiplied greatly in Jerusalem. (Acts 6:7)

Therefore those who were scattered went everywhere preaching
the word. (Acts 8:4)

But the word of God grew and multiplied. (Acts 12:24)

On the next Sabbath almost the whole city came together to hear
the word of God. (Acts 13:44)

And the word of the Lord was being spread throughout all
the region. (Acts 13:49)

Paul and Barnabas also remained in Antioch, teaching and
preaching the word of the Lord, with many others also. (Acts 15:35)

And he continued there a year and six months, teaching the word
of God among them. (Acts 18:11)

And this continued for two years, so that all who dwelt in Asia
heard the word of the Lord Jesus, both Jews and Greeks. (Acts 19:10)

So the word of the Lord grew mightily and prevailed. (Acts 19:20)

So now, brethren, I commend you to God and to the word of His
grace, which is able to build you up and give you an inheritance
among all those who are sanctified. (Acts 20:32)

One requirement of every elder is that he be able to teach *(1 Tim.*
3:2). Paul exhorted Timothy:

And the things that you have heard from me among many witnesses,
commit these to faithful men who will be able to teach others also.
(2 Tim. 2:20)

Handing down good doctrine from generation to generation keeps the church strong. *Psalm*, chapter *119*, stresses over and over how vital good teaching is to believers' lives.

Blessed are the undefiled in the way, who walk in the law of the Lord! (v. 1)

How can a young man cleanse his way? By taking heed according to Your word (v. 9)

Your word I have hidden in my heart, that I might not sin against You! (v. 11)

Your word is a lamp to my feet and a light to my path. (v. 105)

The entrance of Your words gives light; it gives understanding to the simple. (v. 130)

Great peace have those who love Your law, and nothing causes them to stumble. (v. 165)

Christians who enjoy the moving of the Spirit must also develop a love for teaching from the Word of God. The Word makes believers grow. I have been in gatherings considered outstanding because "the Spirit moved and we didn't have time for the preaching." The church needs to return to the New Testament pattern of gatherings centered on the Word.

A pattern church is well-taught. It offers ongoing, systematic teaching of the Bible. Everyone who comes into the house of the

Lord should learn basic doctrine. Members as well as new believers need to know what the church believes and why it does what it does. They must understand the household of faith. Hearing the Scriptures taught, believers grow strong in faith.

Faith comes by hearing, and hearing by the word of God.

(Rom. 10:17)

Many people today read the Bible only to meet emotional needs in a personal crisis. They do not read it to discover truth and understand its doctrine. They read it superficially when they could gain strength from its depth of wisdom.

Winds of false doctrine will blow Christians off course if they do not have a good background in the Word of God. Their faith and commitment to the Word of God sustain them in the day of battle. People who stand for nothing will fall for anything. They are susceptible to being deceived by this evil generation.

Leaders must renew their emphasis on the Word of God. Do not just read it devotionally but study it to learn the ways of God, His plan for your life, and His plan for the Lord's people. A church that is not well taught and giving itself to the apostles' doctrine will not endure the test of time.

THE DOCTRINE OF CHRIST

The apostles' doctrine emphasizes the centrality of Jesus Christ. The doctrine of Christ is the first, last, and central of all truths. He is the Truth. Pastors must continually point to Jesus and lift Him up. Lost souls must be directed to come to Him, and believers must be admonished to abide in Him. Jesus is not *a* hope; He is *the only hope* for this world, so He must remain the central point of all teaching.

> *Did we not strictly command you not to teach in this name? And look, you have filled Jerusalem with your doctrine, and intend to bring this Man's blood on us!* (Acts 5:28)

> *And daily in the temple, and in every house, they did not cease teaching and preaching Jesus Christ.* (Acts 5:42)

> *Immediately he preached the Christ in the synagogues, that He is the Son of God.* (Acts 9:20)

> *Paul and Barnabas also remained in Antioch, teaching and preaching the word of the Lord, with many others also.* (Acts 15:35)

The Bible gives the pattern for balanced Christian living. Congregations fed a diet of basic truths and foundational doctrines are settled and grounded. They are less susceptible to being controlled by feelings or led astray by curiosities. To make it to the end, they need balance.

> *... to present you holy, and blameless, and above reproach in His sight — if indeed you continue in the faith, grounded and steadfast, and are not moved away from the hope of the gospel which you heard.* (Col. 1:22–23)

The Bible says doctrine is like the dew of heaven *(Deut. 32:2)*, yet I heard one critic say, "Doctrine is the greatest curse that ever came to the church."

Critics object to an emphasis on doctrine claiming:

1. **It is divisive.** Critics say doctrine divides the church into denom-

inations. Really, doctrine existed before the church began. God originated it. The church did not. Doctrine is not divisive; people are. The way people use doctrine causes conflict in the body of Christ.

2. *It is irrelevant.* Some say, "What you believe does not matter; what matters is who you believe in." Jesus said, *"False Christs ... will arise"* so when people say they believe in God or in Jesus, which Jesus do they believe in? Where do they get their information about God? Knowing God requires knowing truth — doctrine — about God.

3. *Being right in doctrine is not acceptable to God if you are wrong in spirit, yet being right in spirit while wrong in doctrine is acceptable.* The world is filled with people who are sincere — sincerely wrong! Why not determine to be right in spirit and in doctrine?

4. *Doctrine is dry, dull, dead, useless.* Doctrine is not as exciting as dancing and shouting. It does not draw big crowds like miracles and loud music. But only doctrine builds genuine strength and sustains growth.

Here is a true saying: If you have the Word without the Spirit, you will dry up. If you have the Spirit without the Word, you will blow up. If you have the Spirit and the Word, you will grow up.

Healthy churches with life and power always have a combination and balance of the Spirit and the Word, true to the New Testament pattern. The Bible identifies four sources of doctrine:

1. *The doctrine of God.* This doctrine is refreshing and the foundation for growth. *"Let my teaching drop as the rain, my speech distill as the dew, as raindrops on the tender herb, and as showers on the grass."* (Deut. 32:2)

2. **The doctrine of Christ.** Jesus was accepted as a Rabbi in his day. He was a master teacher. He spoke with authority and clarity. *"And so it was, when Jesus had ended these sayings, that the people were astonished at His teaching, for He taught them as one having authority, and not as the scribes"* (Matt. 7:28–29).

3. **The doctrine of the apostles.** The apostles' doctrine guided the New Testament church. *"They continued steadfastly in the apostles' doctrine"* (Acts 2:42).

4. **The doctrine of devils.** Doctrine can be empowered by evil spirits speaking through evil men. Not all teaching comes from the mind of God. *"Now the Spirit expressly says that in latter times some will depart from the faith, giving heed to deceiving spirits and doctrines of demons"* (1 Tim. 4:1). Believers know the doctrine of devils by discernment and by examining it in the light of the Scripture.

SIX ELEMENTARY DOCTRINES

The apostles' doctrine included six foundational "elementary principles of Christ," according to the book of Hebrews:

> *Therefore, leaving the discussion of the elementary principles of Christ, let us go on to perfection, not laying again the foundation of repentance from dead works and of faith toward God, of the doctrine of baptisms, of laying on of hands, of resurrection of the dead, and of eternal judgment.* (Heb. 6:1–2)

These six doctrines actually involve the following three related pairs of truths: *(a)* repentance and faith, *(b)* baptisms and the laying on of hands, and *(c)* resurrection and eternal judgment. The Jerusalem church experienced all six foundational truths in a measure:

1. Salvation by repentance and faith *(Acts 2:38; 16:30–31)*.
2. Water baptism by immersion *(Acts 2:41; 8:38–39)*.
3. The baptism in the Holy Spirit *(Acts 2:38–39; 10:44–46; 10:2–6)*.
4. Laying on of hands and prophecy *(Acts 13:3)*.
5. Resurrection of the dead *(Acts 9:36–40)*.
6. The judgment of God *(Acts 5:3–6; 13:10–11)*.

Initially, the laying on of hands related primarily to receiving the baptism in the Holy Spirit. However, later, the laying on of hands was used to release the grace and power of God in a variety of contexts. The doctrines of resurrection and eternal judgment have a future fulfillment, but they also cover the new convert's present experience of turning from death to life.

To see the dynamics of the first New Testament church restored, Christians today need to understand and experience the foundational doctrines of Christ. Bible doctrine should be studied because:

1. It gives substance to believers' faith confession.
2. It stabilizes Christians in times of testing.
3. It enables the saints to handle the Bible correctly.
4. It equips the believers to detect and confront error.
5. It makes Christians confident in their walk.
6. It calms their fears and cancels their superstitions.
7. It gives saints objective beliefs that form the foundation of their Christian lives.

With elementary doctrines understood and experienced, Christians can "go on to perfection" or maturity.

A LIFE IN COMMON

As soon as the saints in Jerusalem entered covenant relationship with Jesus, they began associating with each other often. Believers need fellowship with their brothers and sisters. They are not like marbles in a bag — gathered in one place but not bonded together. Rather, they are like pieces of a beautiful puzzle that fit together just right.

Acts 2:42 links fellowship with the apostles' doctrine. The verse could be translated as: "the apostles' fellowship that is a result of the apostles' doctrine." The *Beck New Testament* translates the first part of the verse as: *"They were loyal to what the apostles taught in their fellowship."*[21] The *Living Bible* renders it: *"They joined with the other believers in regular attendance at the apostles' teaching."*[22]

Christians enjoy two dimensions of fellowship: *(1)* fellowship with God, and *(2)* fellowship with man. The basis of Christians' fellowship with each other is their fellowship with the Lord. Believers are to have ongoing communion with Him. Being saved cannot be reduced to mental assent to a doctrinal creed; it involves personal relationship and fellowship with Jesus Christ Himself.

> *God is faithful, by whom you were called into the fellowship of His Son, Jesus Christ our Lord.* (1 Cor. 1:9)

> *The grace of the Lord Jesus Christ, and the love of God, and the communion [fellowship] of the Holy Spirit be with you all.* (2 Cor. 13:14)

> *That which we have seen and heard we declare to you, that you also may have fellowship with us; and truly our fellowship is with the Father and with His Son Jesus Christ.* (1 John 1:3)

The Greek word for fellowship is *koinōnía*. It means association, community, joint participation, intimacy, joint contribution, or a collection. It refers to using something in common.

True *koinōnía* involves: *(1)* all believers, *(2)* dynamics that bind the church together, *(3)* unconditional love and acceptance, *(4)* true honesty with humility, *(5)* restoring fallen and stumbling believers,

(6) wise confession and cleansing, *(7)* heartfelt encouragement and availability, *(8)* open houses and a spirit of hospitality.

On the other hand, the Bible forbids Christians to fellowship with: *(1)* the world, *Eph. 5:11; (2)* Satanic spirits and cults, *1 Cor. 10:20; (3)* unrighteousness, *2 Cor. 10:20; (4)* false religion, *2 Pet. 2; Jude 4;* and *(5)* false doctrine, *Gal. 1:7–10; 2 John 9–11.*

RELATING TO ONE ANOTHER

A simple phrase in the New Testament leads to an understanding of how Christians are to relate together in true fellowship. That phrase is *one another,* the Greek word *allēlous.* Verses that contain this phrase speak of believers lives together and how they are to treat one another.

The basis of their relating to one another is the relationship they have with God. As a result of being washed in the blood of the Lamb they can have true fellowship with one another. They share the most precious things together.

> *But if we walk in the light as He is in the light, we have fellowship with one another, and the blood of Jesus Christ His Son cleanses us from all sin.* (1 John 1:7)

Christians are to fellowship with one another in the following ways:

1. *"Have peace with one another" (Mark 9:50).* In this way we will be salt in the world.
2. *"Be kindly affectionate to one another" (Rom. 12:10).* We are to love one another as members of one family.
3. *"Giving preference to one another" (Rom. 12:10).* We are to prefer others in specific acts of service.
4. *"Be of the same mind toward one another" (Rom. 12:16).* We are to

be unified in values and goals. (See also *Rom. 15:5.*)

5. *"Receive one another" (Rom. 15:7)*. Fully accept one another.

6. *"Admonish one another" (Rom. 15:14)*. Caution one another, reminding each other of the dangers that might lie ahead.

7. *"Greet one another" (Rom. 16:16)*. Embrace one another in a holy welcome. *(See also 1 Cor. 16:20; 2 Cor. 13:12; 1 Pet. 5:14.)*

8. *"Wait for one another" (1 Cor. 11:33)*. We are not to selfishly move ahead of one another.

9. *"Have the same care for one another" (1 Cor. 12:25)*. Treat every member with the same concern and affection.

10. *"Serve one another" (Gal. 5:13)*. We are now free to dedicate ourselves to one another, being a blessing, serving in practical ways. *(See also 1 Pet. 4:10.)* Koinōnía may also have reference to the collection and distribution of gifts. *(cf. Rom. 15:26; 2 Cor. 8:4; 9:13; Heb. 13:16.)*

11. *"Bearing with one another" (Eph. 4:2)*. We are to bear with one another's weaknesses, standing strong in our devotion to one another no matter how offended we might get. *(See also Col. 3:13.)*

12. *"Be kind to one another" (Eph. 4:32)*. Be gracious and easy going with one another.

13. *"Tenderhearted, forgiving one another" (Eph. 4:32)*. We must be filled with compassion for one another, graciously forgiving one another from our hearts. *(See also Col. 3:13.)*

14. *"Speaking to one another in psalms and hymns and spiritual songs" (Eph. 5:19)*. Bring the presence of the Lord into the center of our fellowship. *(See also Col. 3:16.)*

15. *"Submitting to one another" (Eph. 5:21)*. Respect one another and respond to one another with an open heart. *(See also 1 Pet. 5:5.)*

16. *"Comfort one another" (1 Thess. 4:18)*. Stay close to each other and support one another with a word of encouragement in times of crisis or discouragement. *(See also 1 Thess. 5:11; Heb. 3:13; 10:25.)*

17. *"Edify one another" (1 Thess. 5:11)*. Always build each other up and not tear down; be a blessing and not a curse.

18. *"Consider one another in order to stir up love and good works"* (Heb. 10:24). Positively provoke one another to press forward in the will of God.

19. *"Confess your trespasses to one another"* (James 5:16). Be open and honest with each other.

20. *"Pray for one another"* (James 5:16). Stand in the gap for one another in the presence of the Lord.

21. *"Having compassion for one another"* (1 Pet. 3:8). Be sympathetic for one another, identifying with each other at the point of need.

22. *"Be hospitable to one another"* (1 Pet. 4:9). Have a sincere desire to host one another in our homes.

Finally, all of you be of one mind, having compassion for one another; love as brothers, be tenderhearted, be courteous. (1 Pet. 3:8)

The Scripture exhorts believers to avoid the following negative ways of relating:

1. *"Let us not judge one another"* (Rom. 14:13). We are to bless and encourage, not unduly criticize.

2. Do not *"go to law against one another"* (1 Cor. 6:7). Settle differences and conflicts peacefully and among ourselves.

3. Do not *"bite and devour one another ... lest you be consumed by one another"* (Gal. 5:15). Do not tear each other down with words.

4. Do not get involved in *"provoking one another, envying one another"* (Gal. 5:26). Do not let pride create unnecessary conflicts.

5. *"Do not lie to one another"* (Col. 3:9). Do not mislead one another with words.

6. Do not be *"hateful and hating one another"* (Titus 3:3). Do not seek to harm one another.

7. *"Do not speak evil one of another"* (James 4:11). Rather protect and promote one another's good reputation.

8. *"Do not grumble against one another"* (James 5:9). Do not spread discord and complaints throughout the fellowship.

In every case, the commandments and exhortations of Scripture regarding how Christians are to relate to one another can be summed up in one phrase: *Love one another.* Jesus calls and empowers His saints to love each other as He loves us. He asks believers to commit themselves to selflessly pouring out their lives for one another. This is the new law, the law of love.

> *A new commandment I give to you, that you love one another; as I have loved you, that you also love one another. By this all will know that you are My disciples, if you have love for one another.*
> (John 13:34–35)

> *This is My commandment, that you love one another as I have loved you.*
> (John 15:12)

> *And may the Lord make you increase and abound in love to one another and to all, just as we do to you.*
> (1 Thess. 3:12)

> *Since you have purified your souls in obeying the truth through the Spirit in sincere love of the brethren, love one another fervently with a pure heart.*
> (1 Pet. 1:22)

> *Beloved, let us love one another, for love is of God; and everyone who loves is born of God and knows God. He who does not love does not know God, for God is love.*
> (1 John 4:7–8)

All Christians are part of the same body of Christ. They are members of each other. They belong to each other. They have been given to one another by the Lord for mutual love, encouragement and strength.

*... we, being many, are one body in Christ, and individually mem-
bers of one another.* (Rom. 12:5; see also *Eph. 4:25*)

The New Testament apostolic fellowship was not just Sunday religion. It was an entire way of life. It brought Christians together into
the presence of the Lord and then sent them out to a needy world. ✠

STUDY QUESTIONS

1. What does it mean to continue steadfastly in something?

2. What does the term doctrine mean?

3. How would you summarize the importance of the Word of God?

4. What role did the Scripture play in the New Testament church?

5. What was the central message of the apostles' doctrine?

6. Why do some object to the teaching of doctrine?

7. What are the elementary doctrines or principles of Christ?

8. What does fellowship mean?

9. What is the first and most important aspect of fellowship?

10. How would you summarize the kind of relationships Christians are to have in the fellowship?

6 A Worshiping Community

*And they continued steadfastly in ... the
breaking of bread, and in prayers.*   — Acts 2:42

SEEKING THE PRESENCE OF THE LORD CONSUMED THE FIRST Christians. It was their most important activity. In worship, spiritual brothers and sisters celebrated their covenant relationship with the Head of the church.

They were addicted to "the breaking of bread." They were not running a bakery or eating bread in a strange way. This was a special, covenantal experience. In his commentary on the book of Acts, F. F. Bruce translates the breaking of bread as the "regular observance of the Lord's Supper."

Use of the definite article *the* in the original language indicates this was more than fellowship. It was worship that expressed their fellowship. In Jewish culture, the breaking of bread was not simply eating a meal or fellowshiping around a meal. It referred to the prayer of blessing said either before a meal or during a time of prayer and worship. For example:

> *And He took bread, gave thanks and broke it, and gave it to them, saying, "This is My body which is given for you; do this in remembrance of Me."*   (Luke 22:19; see also Matt. 26:26; Mark 14:22)

Now it came to pass, as He sat at the table with them, that He took bread, blessed and broke it, and gave it to them.

(Luke 24:30; see also 24:35)

Now on the first day of the week, when the disciples came together to break bread, Paul, ready to depart the next day, spoke to them and continued his message until midnight. *(Acts 20:7; see also v. 11)*

The same language appears in stories of Jesus supernaturally feeding crowds of 5,000 and 4,000 people.

Then He commanded the multitudes to sit down on the grass. And He took the five loaves and the two fish, and looking up to heaven, He blessed and broke and gave the loaves to the disciples; and the disciples gave to the multitudes.

(Matt. 14:19; see also Matt. 15:32; Mark 8:6, 19)

Passages written by the apostle Paul concerning the Table of the Lord or Communion service use the same language.

The cup of blessing which we bless, is it not the communion of the blood of Christ? The bread which we break, is it not the communion of the body of Christ? *(1 Cor. 10:16)*

... and when He had given thanks, He broke it and said, 'Take, eat; this is My body which is broken for you; do this in remembrance of Me.' *(1 Cor. 11:24)*

The breaking of bread is a time of worship and thanksgiving for the covenant relationship believers have been brought into by the Lord.

A ROYAL PRIESTHOOD

The church fulfills several Old Testament types and symbols. One pictures the congregation of saints as a temple built of stones. Another compares believers to priests who minister in the temple. The apostle Peter calls believers spiritual priests offering spiritual sacrifices in a spiritual sanctuary.

> *Coming to Him as to a living stone, rejected indeed by men, but chosen by God and precious, you also, as living stones, are being built up a spiritual house, a holy priesthood, to offer up spiritual sacrifices acceptable to God through Jesus Christ.* (1 Pet. 2:4–5)

> *But you are a chosen generation, a royal priesthood, a holy nation, His own special people, that you may proclaim the praises of Him who called you out of darkness into His marvelous light; who once were not a people but are now the people of God, who had not obtained mercy but now have obtained mercy.* (1 Pet. 2:9–10)

With spiritual sacrifices and offerings, believer-priests approach the Lord in a new and living way *(Heb. 10:20)*. Sacrifices prescribed in the New Testament pattern include the following:

1. *Physical bodies* "I beseech you therefore, brethren, by the mercies of God, that you present your bodies a living sacrifice, holy, acceptable to God, which is your reasonable service" *(Rom. 12:1)*. Like with the whole burnt offering of the Old Testament, a Christian offers his entire being-spirit, soul and body-to the Lord. The saints belong to Him!

2. *Praise and Thanksgiving* "Therefore by Him let us continually offer the sacrifice of praise to God, that is, the fruit of our lips, giving thanks to His name" *(Heb. 13:15)*. Worshipers' hearts overflow in

true thankfulness and rejoicing in the Lord. Their worship is an offering that gives the Lord great pleasure.

3. **Sharing** *"But do not forget to do good and to share, for with such sacrifices God is well pleased" (Heb. 13:16).* Fellowship between saints and love for one another are sweet to the Lord.

4. **Service** *"If I am being poured out as a drink offering on the sacrifice and service of your faith, I am glad and rejoice with you all" (Phil. 2:17).* The Lord directs worshipers' attention to the serving of others. The love of God is seen as they pour out their lives in practical ways.

5. **Substance** *"Indeed I have all and abound. I am full, having received from Epaphroditus the things sent from you, a sweet-smelling aroma, an acceptable sacrifice, well pleasing to God" (Phil. 4:18).* The Lord calls Christians to put their money where their mouths are. Believers return to the Lord the first, best portion of what He has given to them as a sacred, memorial portion. When given in love, it is accepted as worship, a spiritual sacrifice to the Lord.

Jesus the High Priest oversees His believer-priests as they perform their priestly duties. He made it all possible by His eternal sacrifice. Even now He leads His church in eternal intercession and worship.

Therefore, in all things He had to be made like His brethren, that He might be a merciful and faithful High Priest in things pertaining to God, to make propitiation for the sins of the people.
(Heb. 2:17)

Seeing then that we have a great High Priest who has passed through the heavens, Jesus the Son of God, let us hold fast our confession (Heb. 4:14).

THE TABLE OF THE LORD

As priests of the New Covenant, Christians serve God in a tabernacle that is newer and better than the one Moses built. The Old Testament tabernacle housed a table of showbread. On the table lay the bread of the Presence of God.

Put the bread of the Presence on this table to be before me at all times.   *(Exod. 25:30 NIV)*

The table of showbread symbolized New Testament Communion, also known as the Table of the Lord, the love feast, or the thanksgiving eucharist. Worshipers break the bread. They gather in the presence of the Lord to celebrate the New Covenant meal as a high expression of worship. Jesus had started it, and His followers kept enjoying it week after week.

The Lord calls worshipers to a table of fellowship, worship, celebration, and covenant in His presence. They eat at that table; they experience true satisfaction; their needs are met.

According to the New Testament, Communion or the Lord's Table is as follows:

1. **A time of remembrance**   *"For I received from the Lord that which I also delivered to you: that the Lord Jesus on the same night in which He was betrayed took bread; and when He had given thanks, He broke it and said, 'Take, eat; this is My body which is broken for you; do this in remembrance of Me.' In the same manner He also took the cup after supper, saying, 'This cup is the new covenant in My blood. This do, as often as you drink it, in remembrance of Me'"*

(1 Cor. 11:23–25). Worshipers remember the Lord, Jesus Christ, who He is, what He has done for them, and the life they now have because of Him. They celebrate Jesus!

2. **A time of proclamation** *"For as often as you eat this bread and drink this cup, you proclaim the Lord's death till He comes" (1 Cor. 11:26)*. As they celebrate together, worshipers preach the Gospel to principalities and powers, visitors, and anyone willing to listen.

3. **A time of self-examination** *"Therefore whoever eats this bread or drinks this cup of the Lord in an unworthy manner will be guilty of the body and blood of the Lord. But let a man examine himself, and so let him eat of the bread and drink of the cup. For he who eats and drinks in an unworthy manner eats and drinks judgment to himself, not discerning the Lord's body. For this reason many are weak and sick among you, and many sleep. For if we would judge ourselves, we would not be judged. But when we are judged, we are chastened by the Lord, that we may not be condemned with the world" (1 Cor. 11:27–32)*. It is a time of repentance and cleansing. Worshipers open up their hearts and lives to the Lord in a new way, asking Him to expose the works of darkness and dispel the power of the enemy.

4. **A time of blessing** *"The cup of blessing which we bless, is it not the communion of the blood of Christ? The bread which we break, is it not the communion of the body of Christ?" (1 Cor. 10:16)*. The blessing of the Lord rests upon His people as they worship together in His presence. As they rejoice in Him He gives them His joy, which is their strength.

5. **A time of fellowship and unity** *"For we, though many, are one bread and one body; for we all partake of that one bread" (1 Cor.*

10:17). The Lord binds worshipers' hearts together into one new loaf as they remember and proclaim the broken body of the Lord, turn to Him in true humility and repentance, and receive His blessing. His life draws them together and gives them unity in the Spirit.

Church members who just go through motions of religious ceremony really miss the good Christian life. The church is the dwelling place of God. Intimate communion and fellowship with Him is a priceless privilege and yields great stability in His followers' lives.

DEVOTION TO PRAYER

The Jerusalem church was devoted not only to the breaking of bread but also to prayer. The word translated prayer in the passage means prayer addressed to God or a place set apart for offering prayer. The use of the definite article and the plural noun, *the prayers,* implies specific times of prayer, especially corporate prayer. The use of the simple conjunction and connects these prayer times with "the breaking of bread."

F. F. Bruce states this phrase refers to "their own appointed seasons for united prayer within the new community." [23] R. C. H. Lenski comments that "it seems that this word is used to designate the entire service or worship and not merely the praying." [24] The members of the Jerusalem church had regular "hours of prayer" *(Acts 3:1)* both inside and outside of the temple.

The move of the Holy Spirit stirred the church's devotion to prayer. Every time the church faced a crisis, appointed elders, settled disputes, or made decisions, the church resorted to prayer. Note the following examples:

These all continued with one accord in prayer and supplica-
tion, with the women and Mary the mother of Jesus, and with
His brothers.   *(Acts 1:14)*

When they had prayed, the place where they were assembled
together was shaken; and they were all filled with the Holy Spirit,
and they spoke the word of God with boldness.   *(Acts 4:31)*

We will give ourselves continually to prayer and to the ministry of
the word.   *(Acts 6:4)*

Peter was therefore kept in prison, but constant prayer was offered
to God for him by the church.   *(Acts 12:5)*

At midnight Paul and Silas were praying and singing hymns to
God, and the prisoners were listening to them.   *(Acts 16:25)*

When he had said these things, he knelt down and prayed with
them all.   *(Acts 20:36; see also 21:5)*

Letters from the apostles to young, local churches scattered throughout the Roman Empire contain many admonitions to be "instant" in prayer, or to be "without ceasing" in prayer, or to "continue" in prayer *(see Rom. 12:12; James 5:13; Col. 4:2; 1 Thess. 5:17)*.

The Jerusalem church scheduled specific, special times of corporate prayer that were not considered optional for members. Churches cannot survive without corporate prayer. Praying revived the life of the church I pastored, and whatever brings revival will maintain it.

Ask the Lord for rain in the time of the latter rain. The Lord will
make flashing clouds; he will give them showers of rain, grass in
the field for everyone.   *(Zach. 10:1)*

Western church culture places a fair amount of emphasis on individual prayer but entirely too little on the dynamic and power of corporate prayer. Prayer is a top priority in the New Testament church pattern.

Assuredly, I say to you, whatever you bind on earth will be bound in heaven, and whatever you loose on earth will be loosed in heaven. Again I say to you that if two of you agree on earth concerning anything that they ask, it will be done for them by My Father in heaven. For where two or three are gathered together in My name, I am there in the midst of them. (Matt. 18:18–20)

Jesus' teaching reveals the following elements of corporate prayer:

1. **The power of agreement.** When the people of God are gathered together in unity, even if it is only two or three, the grace of God is released to accomplish the will of God.

2. **The power of the presence of the Lord in the midst of the church.** The Lord dwells in the midst of His people when they gather together in unity. When they are assembled because of His name and because of their faith in and identification with Him, He is present to accomplish His will.

3. **The power to bind the power of sin and darkness.** A unified, worshiping people will tune in to the initiatives of heaven, and heaven and earth will work in concert to see God's rule extended.

4. **The power to remove obstacles to the church.** The power of the presence of the Lord opens doors and makes a way for the unified people of God to do His will. Whatever they loose on earth will have been loosed in heaven.

A HOUSE OF PRAYER

When most believers today use the term prayer, they think of "give me" sessions with a few other saints. They are in a circle or by themselves saying, "Give me, give me, give me, Lord ... thank you Lord ... good-bye." That is all the prayer many believers know.

The prophet Isaiah saw a coming day when all nations would come to God's house for communion. Looking down the corridor of time, he said:

> *The sons of the foreigner who join themselves to the Lord to serve Him ... Even them I will bring to My holy mountain, and make them joyful in My house of prayer. Their burnt offerings and their sacrifices will be accepted on My altar; for My house shall be called a house of prayer for all nations.* (Isa. 56:6–7)

People from all nations will flow into the church. They will enter covenant with the Lord and will find a place of fellowship with Him. His glory will be there. He will meet with them, talk with them, and show them His glory.

Isaiah used the Hebrew word *tĕfillah* for prayer. Five other Hebrew words are translated prayer in the King James Version of the Old Testament, but *tĕfillah* is the most common. It signifies communion taking place in the midst of singing and prayer. Communion with the Lord is a two-way street. The worshiper speaks to the Lord, and the Lord speaks to the worshiper. They have dialogue. In communion, the human spirit and soul express themselves to the Lord.

Tĕfillah appears 76 times in the Old Testament, most often in the book of *Psalms*. According to Young's *Concordance*, it means "songs of praise or hymns."[25] The *Gesenius Lexicon* defines it as "intercession, supplication; a hymn, a sacred song."[26]

Jonah used *tĕfillah* when he offered a sacrifice of praise in the fish's belly.

When my soul fainted within me, I remembered the Lord; and my prayer [těfillah] went up to You, into Your holy temple. "Those who regard worthless idols forsake their own Mercy. But I will sacrifice to You with the voice of thanksgiving; I will pay what I have vowed. Salvation is of the Lord." (Jonah 2:7–9)

His prayer and praise resulted in his immediate deliverance.

Incense in the Old Testament tabernacle and temple symbolized prayer. Incense burned on the gold altar in the Holy Place. To approach God, the high priest took the sweet incense from the gold altar and brought it into the Most Holy Place behind the veil. The aroma of the incense filled the Most Holy Place and surrounded the ark, which was God's dwelling place.

Later, King David interpreted the meaning of the incense saying,

Let my prayer [těfillah] be set before You as incense [and] the lifting up of my hands as the evening sacrifice. (Ps. 141:2)

The great architect of worship and praise, David also compared worshipers' raised hands to the evening sacrifice described in *Exod. 29:41.*

The other five Hebrew words for prayer are as follows:

- *pālal,* to intercede or make supplication. Praying for others is like standing in the gap for them.

- *śiyach,* to ponder, commune or have a conversation. A heart-to-heart conversation with the Lord is appropriate sometimes.

- *'āthar,* to worship, intercede or listen to the Lord. Quiet times in the presence of the Lord are always good.

- *lachash*, to whisper a petition in private. In the privacy of a prayer closet, the saints bring their petitions to Him.

- *chālāh*, to beseech or entreat. Desperation leads Christians to beg the Lord for his mercy at times.

At church, believers from all nations commune with the Lord. They may enjoy one another's company or someone's singing, but the main purpose — even in the music — is to get their minds on the Lord and to commune with Him from beginning to end.

Jesus quotes Isaiah in *Matt. 21:13; Mark 11:17;* and *Luke 19:46.* Paraphrased, Jesus said, *"My house will be a house of communion known by all nations. My saints will enjoy continual fellowship with me. When they come, I will meet with them. They will offer petitions and songs of praise. My voice will be heard in the congregation along with theirs."*

Joy accompanies prayer. Believers enter His presence and make their requests known with thanksgiving. That is why I come. I do not come just to see my buddies. I can meet them at the café.

Satan wants Christians to think prayer is a rigid, gimme, gimme session, where they have to twist God's arm, beg, and plead — and sometimes get what they want. God never meant it to be like that. It is not twisting God's arm; it is communing with the Head of the church.

Many Christians come Sunday morning for worship but are not motivated to attend prayer meetings. Their idea of prayer has been twisted. When the pastor calls the church together for a prayer meeting, little computers in deceived believers' minds announce, "It's an option. It's an option," and only ten percent of the congregation show up.

For any church to succeed, believers must discipline themselves to pray at specific times. When they gather in the house of the Lord, they should focus on Him and share a time of communion with Him. All their attention should focus on Him, not on man.

The Lord's plan for His church is not just to take a bunch of people to heaven. He wants to express His glory on *terra firma*. He wants this earth to see His glory through His body in every community. The church has to come together in unity to touch the community. Everyone in the church must aim toward the same goal.

If some think, "The goal of the church is to have a quartet," then they will focus on developing the ministry of the quartet, thinking that music is the instrument God is using to show forth His glory in the earth. But He has not chosen to do that. God is building His church to be a place of communion for all nations.

COMMUNION IN THE HOUSE

God wants to commune with His spiritual sons and daughters in His house just as human fathers and mothers want to commune with their children at home. The house is for communion between family members.

How would you feel if the following events happened in your home?

After working out of town a couple of weeks, you discover you can arrive home a day earlier than expected. Eagerly, you anticipate seeing and surprising your beautiful wife and children.

So you make the trip, walk up the front sidewalk to your house, open the door and say, "Honey, I'm home!" and you hear no response.

"Dear, I'm here!" you repeat, and again no response.

"Kids, it's your Dad!"

You hear a little noise in the kitchen, walk in there, and see your wife ironing clothes. You say, "Hi, Honey! I came home a day early! It's sure good to be home. Two weeks is a long time."

She looks up and says, "Oh, good. Glad you're home."

"Sure good to see you, Honey! How's everything?"

"Fine."

"I sure missed you, Honey."

"Yeah, I missed you, too."

"Everything okay?"

"Yup."

"Missed me?"

"Yup."

"Nothing wrong?"

"Nope."

"You want to sit down and talk a little bit?"

"Can't you see I'm busy ironing your clothes and cooking this meal! Wait until I get done." "Where are the children?"

"They're watching television in the front room." You walk to the front room, and there are your children sitting on the floor watching television. You say, "Hi, kids! Dad's home!"

"Oh, hi Dad."

"Everything okay?"

"Yup."

"I sure missed you kids."

"Missed you too, Dad."

"Everything going okay around here?"

"Yup."

You walk back into the kitchen. "Everything okay, Honey?"

"Yeah, I told you everything's okay. Don't bother me! I'm busy! I've got to clean up here. I've got all kinds of important things to do. Can't you see I'm busy working for you? Later we can talk — maybe later."

If you encountered that scene every time you came home, your heart would begin to ache. Your wife may keep house well. She may fix the best meals, iron your clothes, and take good care of you and the kids, but she is so busy. You have no communion with her, and your children could not care less.

Would you begin to react and say, "What's wrong around here? What's the matter? You don't talk to me anymore. You don't commune with me anymore."?

"I'm busy. You know that I'm busy."

"I don't care if you're busy; we need communion!"

If she and the kids continued to have that attitude over any length of time, would you feel like kicking the house down and starting over? I bought our home when I was in my twenties. I worked hard, saved a down payment, bought the home and moved into it. I took the wife of my youth into that home to love her and commune with her. Out of our loving relationship came the children. But if everyone got too busy and there was no communion in the home, then the house would mean nothing to me.

The Lord declared through Isaiah the prophet, "The day is coming when My house will be a house of communion for everyone, and they all will enjoy fellowship in My house." In Jesus' day, the business of money-changing and selling doves for ritual sacrifice had choked spiritual life in the temple. Twice He drove the merchants out of the temple to restore it to a place of prayer and communion with God.

> *So they came to Jerusalem. And Jesus went into the temple and began to drive out those who bought and sold in the temple, and overturned the tables of the moneychangers and the seats of those who sold doves. And He would not allow anyone to carry wares through the temple. Then He taught, saying to them, "Is it not written, 'My house shall be called a house of prayer for all nations'? But you have made it a 'den of thieves'."* (Mark 11:15–17)

Jesus drove the moneychangers out with a whip He had made (*John 2:15*). This quiet man of Galilee who stood and taught so gently, who gathered little children in His arms, touched the wounded, hurting, and sick, all of a sudden showed uncharacteristic zeal in the house of God. He was upset with the Pharisees. He called them snakes, foxes, and whitewashed tombs.

Here was the meek man of Galilee who did not open His mouth when they spit on Him and plucked His beard out, who was like a lamb led to the slaughter, who never responded when they drove the nails into His hand. All through His life He was nonviolent, yet all of a sudden He became forceful. He had a whip. He kicked over tables. Pigeons flew out of their cages. Money rolled down the aisle. People scrambled as Jesus drove them out.

He never resorted to force except in His house. As He did, He said, "My house is for communion with the Father and you have turned it into something it was not intended to be. You have made it a den of thieves for your own profit." If anyone wants to see the Lord's zeal, just use His house the wrong way.

When Jesus cleansed the temple in *Matt. 21:13*, He called it "my house." However by *Matt. 23:38* Jesus called it "your house." Finally, in *Matt. 24:1* the nation had forgotten the purpose of the church, so the glory departed as Jesus departed — Ichabod.

God created men primarily for a loving relationship. The true church Christ is building will be a house of prayer and relationship with God.

A HOUSE OF PRAISE

The Jerusalem church blended praise with prayer. Believers carried a pattern of worship from the Old Testament into the church. The apostle Paul denied accusations that Christian worship broke with Old Testament practices.

> *But this I confess to you, that according to the Way which they call a sect, so I worship the God of my fathers, believing all things which are written in the Law and in the Prophets.* (Acts 24:14)

Paul did not mean early Christians offered animal sacrifices. He meant that they followed the worship pattern established by King

David. The *Psalms* reveal the Davidic pattern. Note references to David and *Psalms* in the epistles and *Acts*.

> *And do not be drunk with wine, in which is dissipation; but be filled with the Spirit, speaking to one another in psalms and hymns and spiritual songs, singing and making melody in your heart to the Lord, giving thanks always for all things to God the Father in the name of our Lord Jesus Christ.* (Eph. 5:18–20)

> *Let the word of Christ dwell in you richly in all wisdom, teaching and admonishing one another in psalms and hymns and spiritual songs, singing with grace in your hearts to the Lord.*
> (Col. 3:16; see also Acts 1:16, 20; 2:25, 29, 34; 4:25; 7:45; 13:22, 34, 36.)

James, the brother of Jesus, agreed to the continued use of Davidic worship patterns in the church. In settling an argument before the elders in Jerusalem, James quoted the prophet Amos:

> *After this I will return and will rebuild the tabernacle of David, which has fallen down; I will rebuild its ruins, and I will set it up.*
> (Acts 15:16; see Amos 9:11)

Amos' prophecy supported the idea that new Gentile believers do not have to enter the Abrahamic and Mosaic Covenants before they can participate in the New Covenant, James said. Amos implied the Davidic Messiah would establish a New Covenant with new spiritual realities for people of all ethnic groups.

Before David's reign, worship centered around the ark in the tabernacle of Moses, but wicked priests under King Saul had taken the ark out of the tabernacle. The ark symbolized the presence of God. Without the ark, tabernacle rituals were empty religious forms. The presence of God was not there.

David, a man after God's own heart, could not tolerate life without the presence of God. After he conquered and occupied Jerusalem, he brought the ark into the city. He did not return the ark to the tabernacle Moses built. Instead, he pitched a new tent on Mount Zion for the ark. Essentially, he established a new Holy of Holies minus the furniture, curtains, and framework that surrounded it in the first tabernacle. (See *2 Sam. 6* and *1 Chron. 13, 15–16* for the complete story.)

The significant difference in the new tent, known as the tabernacle of David, was that during David's reign, everyone in his generation — not only the priests — had equal access to the presence of the Lord. God also revealed to David a new pattern of praise and worship to surround the ark, and David instituted it.

Thus all Israel brought up the ark of the covenant of the LORD
with shouting and with the sound of the horn, with trumpets and
with cymbals, making music with stringed instruments and harps.
(1 Chron. 15:28)

And he appointed some of the Levites to minister before the ark of
the LORD*, to commemorate, to thank, and to praise the* LORD *God*
of Israel. *(1 Chron. 16:4)*

Oh, give thanks to the LORD*! Call upon His name; make known*
His deeds among the peoples! Sing to Him, sing psalms to Him;
talk of all His wondrous works! *(1 Chron. 16:8–9)*

The book of *Psalms* fully develops the pattern David established around the ark. Mount Zion, the site of the tabernacle of David, foreshadowed the New Testament church.

For you have not come to the mountain that may be touched and
that burned with fire, and to blackness and darkness and tempest ...

but you have come to Mount Zion and to the city of the living God, the heavenly Jerusalem, to an innumerable company of angels, to the general assembly and church of the firstborn. *(Heb. 12:18, 22, 23)*

DAVIDIC WORSHIP

The new order of worship God revealed to David begins with preparation of each worshiper's heart. The Lord looks on each heart *(2 Sam. 16:7)*. He is concerned about how people come into His presence. Times of corporate prayer before worship services allow worshipers to prepare their hearts. David discovered that "clean hands and a pure heart" are needed.

Who may ascend into the hill of the Lord? Or who may stand in His holy place? He who has clean hands and a pure heart, who has not lifted up his soul to an idol, nor sworn deceitfully. He shall receive blessing from the Lord, and righteousness from the God of his salvation. *(Ps. 24:3–5)*

The pattern of worship and praise revealed to David includes vocal praise and involvement of the worshiper's entire body. Praise is not silent, mystical, or otherworldly. It is not passive or introverted. It is a real-life expression that comes from the heart and is expressed by the mouth and body posture. Silence always signified death or impending judgment in the *Psalms*.

I cried to the LORD with my voice, and He heard me from His holy hill. *(Ps. 3:4)*

My voice You shall hear in the morning, O LORD; in the morning I will direct it to You, and I will look up. *(Ps. 5:3)*

In my distress I called upon the LORD, and cried out to my God;
he heard my voice from His temple, and my cry came before Him,
even to His ears.
      (Ps. 18:6; see also 28:2; 55:17; 66:8; 77:1; 109:30; 130:2; 141:1; 142:1; 149:6)

The dead do not praise the LORD, nor any who go down
into silence.   *(Ps. 115:17)*

Vocal praise includes:

Singing   According to Paul, praise involves psalms, hymns, and spiritual songs. All songs of praise — old and new, established and spontaneous — are worship to the Lord. *"Sing praises to God, sing praises! Sing praises to our King, sing praises!" (Ps. 47:6).*

Shouting   *"Be glad in the LORD and rejoice, you righteous; and shout for joy, all you upright in heart!" (Ps. 32:11).* Shouting provides a note of triumph, rejoicing in the victory of the Lord.

Bodily actions in worship include:

Clapping   *"Clap your hands, all you peoples! Shout to God with the voice of triumph!" (Ps. 47:1).* Like shouting, clapping expresses victory and intimidates the enemy.

Standing   *"Bless the LORD, all you servants of the LORD, who by night stand in the house of the LORD!" (Ps. 134:1).* Standing expresses respect and readiness in the presence of the Lord.

Lifting hands   *"Lift up your hands in the sanctuary, and bless the LORD" (Ps. 134:2).* Lifted hands express love, surrender, and receptivity to the Lord.

Kneeling and bowing   *"Oh come, let us worship and bow down; let us kneel before the LORD our Maker" (Ps. 95:6).* A kneeling worshiper humbles himself before the Lord in submission and surrender.

Playing musical instruments   *"Praise Him with the sound of the trumpet; praise Him with the lute and harp! Praise Him with the timbrel and dance; praise Him with stringed instruments and flutes! Praise*

Him with loud cymbals; praise Him with clashing cymbals!" (Ps. 150:3–5). The word translated psalm in both Old and New Testaments means a song of praise accompanied by a musical instrument. Music was invented by the Lord to give a full range of expression, including worship of its Creator.

Dancing *"Let them praise His name with the dance; let them sing praises to Him with the timbrel and harp" (Ps. 149:3; see 30:11; 150:4).* Dancing is a natural human expression of joy and rejoicing. Why not express those feelings toward the Lord?

The *Psalms* give the following reasons to praise the Lord:

- **God commands it.** *"You who fear the LORD, praise Him! All you descendants of Jacob, glorify Him, and fear Him, all you offspring of Israel!" (Ps. 22:23).*
- **He is worthy to be praised.** *"I will call upon the LORD, who is worthy to be praised; so shall I be saved from my enemies" (Ps. 18:3).* Worshipers praise the Lord because He deserves it. They do not praise Him because they feel like it or even because He has blessed them.
- **It is the ordained way of entering His presence.** *"Enter into His gates with thanksgiving, and into His courts with praise. Be thankful to Him, and bless His name" (Ps. 100:4).*
- **It is the way believers glorify God.** *"Whoever offers praise glorifies Me; and to him who orders his conduct aright I will show the salvation of God" (Ps. 50:23).*
- **It proclaims the goodness of God to others.** *"He has put a new song in my mouth — praise to our God; many will see it and fear, and will trust in the Lord" (Ps. 40:3).*
- **It releases the power of his presence.** *"But You are holy, enthroned in the praises of Israel" (Ps. 22:3).* The NASB translates this verse, *"Yet Thou art holy, O Thou who art enthroned upon the praises of Israel."*[27] The Lord inhabits the praises of His people. He is enthroned on their praises, and in such a circumstance

His power can be released in a special way to accomplish His will. (For examples of how this works, see *2 Chron. 20:1–22* and *Acts 16:25–26*.)

- *It transforms the worshiper.* People become like the object of their worship. *"Those who make them are like them; so is everyone who trusts in them" (Ps. 115:8).* Christians are transformed in the presence of the Lord.

But we all, with unveiled face, beholding as in a mirror the glory of the Lord, are being transformed into the same image from glory to glory, just as by the Spirit of the Lord.　　　　　　(2 Cor. 3:18)

THE GLORY OF THE LORD

Glory is a manifestation of God's presence. Worshipers seek the presence of the Lord, and their hearts hunger for a glimpse of His face.

As the deer pants for the water brooks, so pants my soul for You, O God. My soul thirsts for God, for the living God. When shall I come and appear before God?　　　　　　(Ps. 42:1–2)

When worshipers get excited in the house of the Lord they say, "Glory!" What they really are saying is, "The Lord is here! He is doing wonderful things! He is meeting me! He is touching me! He is real to me!" They are expressing the fact that the Lord Jesus is present in the church.

Unto Him be glory in the church. (Eph. 3:21)

In his dialogue with the Lord, Moses asked to see the glory of God.

And He said, "My Presence will go with you, and I will give you rest." Then he said to Him, "If Your Presence does not go with us, do not bring us up from here. For how then will it be known that Your people and I have found grace in Your sight, except You go with us? So we shall be separate, Your people and I, from all the people who arc upon the face of the earth." So the Lord said to Moses, "I will also do this thing that you have spoken; for you have found grace in My sight, and I know you by name." And he said, "Please, show me Your glory."　　　　　　　　*(Exod. 33:14–18)*

The Lord wants to manifest His presence in the church. That is why unity in the body of Christ is important. He reveals His presence in His united body. Paul wrote, *"Christ in you* [plural], *the hope of glory" (Col. 1:27).* You is not singular. It does not state, "Christ in me, my expression of His presence." The verse speaks of the church. It could be paraphrased as: *"Christ in you all — the church — is the hope of a present manifestation of His presence."* The church together, in order, in unity praising the Lord, manifests His presence.

Many people read this verse to say, "Christ in you, the hope of going to heaven", but that is not what Paul said.

When worshipers are in God's presence, He moves toward man. He blesses. He heals. He gives words of wisdom. He answers questions by prophecy or by the preaching of the Word. Coming and going in the house of God is a joyful experience. To come into the presence of God is true joy and satisfaction!

You will show me the path of life; in Your presence is fullness of joy; at Your right hand are pleasures forevermore.　(Ps. 16:11)　✠

STUDY QUESTIONS

1. What does the phrase *breaking of bread* refer to?

2. What are five New Testament sacrifices?

3. What do *the prayers* refer to?

4. What was the role of prayer in the New Testament church?

5. What is the significance of corporate prayer?

6. What is the *table of the Lord*?

7. How is the church a house of prayer?

8. Why is David significant to the pattern of praise and worship in the New Testament church?

9. How are Christians to praise the Lord?

10. What is the glory of the Lord? How is it to be seen in the church?

7 *Awesome Signs*

S UPERNATURAL SIGNS AND WONDERS REVEALED GOD'S presence in the early church. Through miracles, God gave tangible, visible evidence that He, who is supernatural, was in fact present. Miraculous signs occurred frequently. They were part of the ongoing, normal lifestyle of the church. The testimony of signs and wonders created a healthy fear of the Lord and a sense of wonder in people. God used miracles and wonders to authenticate the men He sent and to prove their message was His own. Miracles also commanded the attention of people outside of the church.

> *God also bearing witness both with signs and wonders, with various miracles, and gifts of the Holy Spirit, according to His own will.* (Heb. 2:4)

The word *wonders* describes an event or object so strange that people stop to watch or observe it. It is a prodigy or a portent. In Greek manuscripts of the New Testament, *wonders* is found only in plural and in combination with the word *signs*. The word translated signs means a mark or token that distinguishes a person or thing from others. Signs also can portend remarkable events soon to happen.

The phrase *signs and wonders* appears 16 times in the New Testament, nine times in the book of *Acts (2:19, 22, 43; 4:30; 5:12; 6:8; 7:36; 14:3; 15:12. See also Matt. 24:24; Mark 13:22; John 4:48; Rom. 15:19; 2 Cor. 12:12; 2 Thess. 2:9.)* Acts 2:43 begins a series of verbs in the imperfect tense, which attest to the continual activity in miracles.

God gave signs and wonders to the church as gifts. They were inseparable from the life and preaching of the church. They were an integral part of the mission of the church. Without the supernatural, Jesus Christ would not have been born and lived among men. Without the supernatural, the New Testament church would not have begun. Without the supernatural, Christianity would not exist. The New Covenant people of God are called to be supernatural people in every area of life.

> *And through the hands of the apostles many signs and wonders were done among the people.* (Acts 5:12)

> *And Stephen, full of faith and power, did great wonders and signs among the people.* (Acts 6:8)

> *Therefore they stayed there a long time, speaking boldly in the Lord, who was bearing witness to the word of His grace, granting signs and wonders to be done by their hands.* (Acts 14:3)

The supernatural presence and power of God was evident in the following variety of ways:

Healing The church ministered supernatural healing to people. As a result, the Word of God spread as it would not have otherwise.

> *And Peter said to him, "Aeneas, Jesus the Christ heals you. Arise and make your bed." Then he arose immediately. So all who dwelt at Lydda and Sharon saw him and turned to the Lord.* (Acts 9:34–35)

*This man heard Paul speaking. Paul, observing him intently
and seeing that he had faith to be healed, said with a loud voice,
"Stand up straight on your feet!" And he leaped and walked.*

(Acts 14:9–10)

*The father of Publius lay sick of a fever and dysentery. Paul went
in to him and prayed, and he laid his hands on him and healed
him. So when this was done, the rest of those on the island who
had diseases also came and were healed.*

(Acts 28:8–9; see also 3:6; 8:6–7)

Healing included raising people from the dead.

*But Peter put them all out, and knelt down and prayed. And
turning to the body he said, 'Tabitha, arise.' And she opened her
eyes, and when she saw Peter she sat up. Then he gave her his hand
and lifted her up; and when he had called the saints and widows,
he presented her alive. And it became known throughout all Joppa,
and many believed on the Lord.* (Acts 9:40–42)

Deliverance   God supernaturally delivered saints from difficult
circumstances. Often angels participated in the deliverance.

*But at night an angel of the Lord opened the prison doors and
brought them out.* (Acts 5:19)

*Now behold, an angel of the Lord stood by him, and a light shone
in the prison; and he struck Peter on the side and raised him up,
saying, 'Arise quickly!' And his chains fell off his hands.* (Acts 12:7)

But he shook off the creature into the fire and suffered no harm.

(Acts 28:5)

God also delivered people from evil spirits. Believers confronted the kingdom of darkness and cast out demons.

> *And this she did for many days. But Paul, greatly annoyed, turned and said to the spirit, "I command you in the name of Jesus Christ to come out of her." And he came out that very hour.* (Acts 16:18)

Prophecy The Lord gave the saints supernatural messages, including dreams and prophecies. As they ministered to the Lord and fasted, the Holy Spirit said, 'Now separate to Me Barnabas and Saul for the work to which I have called them' *(Acts 13:2;* see also *21:10).*

> *And a vision appeared to Paul in the night. A man of Macedonia stood and pleaded with him, saying, "Come over to Macedonia and help us."* (Acts 16:9; see also 18:9; 23:11; 27:23)

Transport Philip even received supernatural transport from the Judean desert to the city of Caesarea on the coast.

> *Now when they came up out of the water, the Spirit of the Lord caught Philip away, so that the eunuch saw him no more; and he went on his way rejoicing.* (Acts 8:39)

Unusual Miracles The Lord tailored miracles to meet peculiar circumstances in specific places. Customized miracles clearly demonstrated God's power and authority in unique conditions.

> *Now God worked unusual miracles by the hands of Paul, so that even handkerchiefs or aprons were brought from his body to the sick, and the diseases left them and the evil spirits went out of them.* (Acts 19:11–12)

Judgment   Supernatural judgments took place, resulting in an even greater fear of the Lord.

> *Then Ananias, hearing these words, fell down and breathed his last. So great fear came upon all those who heard these things.*
> *(Acts 5:5)*

> *"And now, indeed, the hand of the Lord is upon you, and you shall be blind, not seeing the sun for a time." And immediately a dark mist fell on him, and he went around seeking someone to lead him by the hand.*
> *(Acts 13:11)*

> *Then immediately an angel of the Lord struck him, because he did not give glory to God. And he was eaten by worms and died. But the word of God grew and multiplied.*
> *(Acts 12:23–24)*

The church was not passive about the miraculous. Believers prayed and interceded, asking the Lord to release signs and wonders in their midst.

> *Now, Lord, look on their threats, and grant to Your servants that with all boldness they may speak Your word, by stretching out Your hand to heal, and that signs and wonders may be done through the name of Your holy Servant Jesus.*
> *(Acts 4:29–30)*

The twentieth century western church understands very little about miracles. In fact, modernism denies the possibility of genuine miracles. In contrast, the Jerusalem church saw heaven's constant involvement in the affairs of men. Because the first Christians were more aware of heaven's involvement, they were more effectively involved as partners with heaven in carrying out their mission.

THE DOCTRINE OF MIRACLES

The truth and dynamics of the New Testament church are being restored, including the working of miracles. A miracle is a supernatural event that breaks into the natural. It is the spiritual breaking into the material.

One Greek word translated *miracle* is *dúnamis*. This word is used 113 times in the New Testament. It means inherent power or the power residing in a thing by virtue of its nature. It refers to God's energy, power, ability, influence, wealth, or might. It is translated in the *King James Version* as "power(s)" (77 times); "mighty" or "mightily" (13 times); "miracle(s)" (8 times); "strength" (7 times); "virtue" (3 times); "ability" (1 time); "wonderful" (1 time); "violence" (1 time); "meaning" (1 time); and "abundance" (1 time).

The New Testament church carried on its mission in the power of the Holy Spirit. This pattern will continue until the second coming of Christ, according to the Bible. Spiritual power will increase greatly before the Lord's advent. The church will move in great power, and so will the kingdom of darkness. Therefore, believers will need to distinguish God's miracles from other miracles. People attracted to spiritual power just for the sake of power open themselves to delusion and deception.

Key passages using *dúnamis* include:

These have power to shut heaven, so that no rain falls in the days of their prophecy; and they have power over waters to turn them to blood, and to strike the earth with all plagues, as often as they desire. (Rev. 11:6)

The coming of the lawless one is according to the working of Satan, with all power, signs, and lying wonders. (2 Thess. 2:9)

Another important word pertaining to miracles is the Greek word *sēmeîon*. It refers to a distinguishing mark by which something is known or a visual sign by which something is recognized. It is used 61 times in the New Testament. It is translated in the *King James Version* "sign(s)" (34 times); "miracle(s)" (22 times); "wonder(s)" (3 times); "token" (1 time); and "tare" (1 time).

John uses *sēmeîon* in his Gospel to refer to miracles that are signs of Christ or that reveal something about Christ's nature. For John, miracles always pointed to something about Christ as King or about His kingdom.

> *Then those men, when they had seen the sign that Jesus did, said, "This is truly the Prophet who is to come into the world."* (John 6:14)

> *For this reason the people also met Him, because they heard that He had done this sign.* (John 12:18)

Signs never are an end in themselves. They are signposts, prophetic markers, or supernatural revelations of something beyond themselves. In the New Testament they were signs that the kingdom of God had come. For instance:

- Jesus turned the water into wine *(John 2:1–11)* and then cleansed the temple *(2:12–25)*, demonstrating that the New Covenant era had come.
- Jesus fed the 5,000 *(John 6:1–15)* and then revealed Himself as the Bread of Life *(6:25–59)*.
- Jesus healed a man born blind *(John 9:1–7)* and revealed Himself as the Light of the World *(9:5)*.
- Jesus raised Lazarus from the dead *(John 11:38–44)* and revealed Himself as the Resurrection and the Life *(11:25)*.

People who sought miraculous signs as an end in themselves were condemned by the Lord. They sought miracles for self-centered reasons or for personal blessing. Bored religious people even sought signs for entertainment.

A third Greek word referring to the miraculous is *ergon*. It refers to a deed, action, or accomplishment. It describes something brought into being by work. It is used 177 times in the New Testament and is usually translated "work(s)" or "deed(s)" in the *King James Version*. This word clearly shows that the work of God includes miracles.

For the Father loves the Son, and shows Him all things that He Himself does; and He will show Him greater works than these, that you may marvel. (John 5:20)

But I have a greater witness than John's; for the works which the Father has given Me to finish — the very works that I do — bear witness of Me, that the Father has sent Me. (John 5:36)

Neither this man nor his parents sinned, but that the works of God should be revealed in him. I must work the works of Him who sent Me while it is day; the night is coming when no one can work. (John 9:3–4)

The work and words of God are related. Every work has within it a word. Every miracle has a message. Miracles encourage people to believe the message.

Do you not believe that I am in the Father, and the Father in Me? The words that I speak to you I do not speak on My own authority; but the Father who dwells in Me does the works. Believe Me that I am in the Father and the Father in Me, or else believe Me for the sake of the works themselves. (John 14:10–11)

Jesus promised that the pattern of ministering the work and words of God would increase in the church.

Most assuredly, I say to you, he who believes in Me, the works that I do he will do also; and greater works than these he will do, because I go to My Father.   *(John 14:12)*

In times of revival, the Holy Spirit renews supernatural and miraculous manifestations in the church. Then the Word of the Lord comes and clarifies the meaning and purpose of the miracles. The Word restores the church and enables it to fulfill its mission in the present generation by the power of the Holy Spirit.

Miraculous works of God occur internally and externally. The greatest miracle takes place internally as the Lord changes the hearts of men and forms the image of Christ in them. The power of God works to strengthen Christians to carry out the mission He has given them.

[God] is able to do exceedingly abundantly above all that we ask or think, according to the power that works in us.   *(Eph. 3:20)*

... strengthened with all might, according to His glorious power, for all patience and longsuffering with joy.   *(Col. 1:11)*

Externally, miraculous signs and wonders of God confirm the preaching of the Gospel, making the message more persuasive. The external working of God's power always serves the harvest.

And they went out and preached everywhere, the Lord working with them and confirming the word through the accompanying signs.   *(Mark 16:20)*

But you shall receive power when the Holy Spirit has come upon you; and you shall be witnesses to Me in Jerusalem, and in all Judea and Samaria, and to the end of the earth. (Acts 1:8)

GOD INITIATES & MAN COOPERATES

The obedience of man combines with the will of God to produce miracles. Only God in heaven initiates miracles, but they become reality as believers cooperate with heaven by faith. The sequence of events appears as follows:

1. **Hearing the Word of God.** When believers have ears to hear what the Spirit is saying, they can respond obediently to the Word and see the grace and power of God released to do His will.

   And Ananias went his way and entered the house; and laying his hands on him he said, "Brother Saul, the Lord Jesus, who appeared to you on the road as you came, has sent me that you may receive your sight and be filled with the Holy Spirit." Immediately there fell from his eyes something like scales, and he received his sight at once; and he arose and was baptized. (Acts 9:17–18)

2. **Believing the Word.** When believers hear the Word, they must receive it and be willing to act upon it, no matter how silly they might think it looks.

   And in Lystra a certain man without strength in his feet was sitting, a cripple from his mother's womb, who had never walked. This man heard Paul speaking. Paul, observing him intently and seeing that he had faith to be healed, said with a loud voice, "Stand up straight on your feet!" And he leaped and walked. (Acts 14:8–10)

3. **Speaking the Word.** God's power flows through his Word (see *Gen. 1:2*). Whenever God desires to perform a miracle, He seeks an instrument through which He can speak or articulate His Word. With the speaking of the Word, power is released.

> *Then Peter said, "Silver and gold I do not have, but what I do have I give you: In the name of Jesus Christ of Nazareth, rise up and walk." And he took him by the right hand and lifted him up, and immediately his feet and ankle bones received strength. So he, leaping up, stood and walked and entered the temple with them — walking, leaping, and praising God.* (Acts 3:6–8)

4. **Acting on the Word.** An action must correspond to the Word. A step of faith begins the process of seeing God's sovereign will accomplished.

> *"And now I urge you to take heart, for there will be no loss of life among you, but only of the ship. For there stood by me this night an angel of the God to whom I belong and whom I serve, saying, 'Do not be afraid, Paul; you must be brought before Caesar; and indeed God has granted you all those who sail with you.' Therefore take heart, men, for I believe God that it will be just as it was told me"... Paul said to the centurion and the soldiers, "Unless these men stay in the ship, you cannot be saved." Then the soldiers cut away the ropes of the skiff and let it fall off.* (Acts 27:22–25, 31–32)

Jerusalem Christians sought miracles with faith and proper motives. They were not seeking money *(Acts 8:18)*, a demonstration of human power *(Acts 14:11–15)*, or a hypocritical ritual *(Acts 19:13–16)*.

Miracles happened as believers tapped into the mind of the Lord, walked in it, and acted in faith — not presumption.

PURPOSE OF MIRACLES

The purposes of miracles are as follows:

1. *The deliverance and preservation of God's people based on His love and compassion for them.* Ten times the Gospels say Jesus was moved with compassion. Miracles testify to God's love and covenant relationship with His people.

   > *And Jesus, moved with compassion, put out His hand and touched him, and said to him, "I am willing; be cleansed."*
   > *(Mark 1:41)*

2. *The encouragement of real faith, in believers and unbelievers.* The manifested power of God always causes men to stand in awe and have a healthy fear of God. Faith is sometimes built upon this kind of experiential knowledge.

   > *So great fear came upon all the church and upon all who heard these things.* *(Acts 5:11)*

   Jesus' miracles validated His message and His identity.

   > *Believe Me that I am in the Father and the Father in Me, or else believe Me for the sake of the works themselves.*
   > *(John 14:11)*

3. *Miracles* accompany evangelism and the preaching of the Gospel. Miracles are part of the Great Commission.

And these signs will follow those who believe: In My name they will cast out demons; they will speak with new tongues; they will take up serpents; and if they drink anything deadly, it will by no means hurt them; they will lay hands on the sick, and they will recover. (Mark 16:17–18)

Dúnamis is given to dynamite people in the kingdom of God. When men believe the message of Christ and see miracles, the Father is glorified in and through the Son.

Signs and wonders have not ceased from the church. The Word still needs confirming. Society still needs to know that the kingdom of God has come, and the members of the church have an ongoing need to see the demonstration of God's power. Signs and wonders are basic essentials of church life.

A SUPERNATURALLY GIFTED CHURCH

The nine gifts listed in *1 Corinthians* chapter *12*, are the basic supernatural manifestations of the Holy Spirit. They are direct manifestations given to believers.

For to one is given the word of wisdom through the Spirit, to another the word of knowledge through the same Spirit, to another faith by the same Spirit, to another gifts of healings by the same Spirit, to another the working of miracles, to another prophecy, to another discerning of spirits, to another different kinds of tongues, to another the interpretation of tongues. (1 Cor. 12:8–10)

God may equip everyone by personality and temperament to match the gifts He gives them, yet the function of gifts goes beyond the personality and ability of men. The Holy Spirit's supernatural influence makes the gifts operate.

Paul described the proper attitude believers should have toward the gifts of the Spirit:

- Be knowledgeable. Christians are not to be ignorant of spiritual gifts. They need to think through what these manifestations of the Spirit are and how they are to be used. Each believer also should consider how he can be used to express them.

  Now concerning spiritual gifts, brethren, I do not want you to be ignorant. (1 Cor. 12:1)

- Recognize your own gift. Every believer has the potential to function in at least one gift. He receives it for the good of the entire church, not for his own gratification.

  But the manifestation of the Spirit is given to each one for the profit of all. (1 Cor. 12:7)

  All believers have the Holy Spirit operating in them. All have the ability to move in the supernatural, "but one and the same Spirit works all these things, distributing to each one individually as He wills." (1 Cor. 12:11)

- Desire the gifts needed in a particular church. A Christian's motivation should be love and a desire to bless others. If love is weak, the gifts will not edify or have their full effect. The fruit of the Spirit and love endows gifts with full authority and power to minister grace to others.

  But earnestly desire the best gifts. (1 Cor. 12:31)

- Stir up the gifts. Believers should not neglect their gifts but stir them up. Saints are stewards over the gifts.

Therefore I remind you to stir up the gift of God which is in you through the laying on of my hands. (2 Tim. 1:6)

- Guard against misuse and abuse. Once God gives a gift, it will not be withdrawn or recalled.

The gifts and the calling of God are irrevocable. (Rom. 11:29)

To avoid misuse or abuse of the gifts, they must remain submitted to the written Word of God. A man may be convinced he has a revelation or word from the Lord, but if it contradicts the clear teaching of Scripture, it must not be accepted. The church's only safeguard from delusion is to stay within the boundaries of objective, revealed truth from the Bible.

If anyone thinks himself to be a prophet or spiritual, let him acknowledge that the things which I write to you are the commandments of the Lord. (1 Cor. 14:37)

Leaders of local churches also oversee the operation of the gifts. The fact that gifts are spiritual does not mean they cannot be ordered, guided, and judged. God knows the potential for human error always exists, and He has provided for its restraint and correction.

Let two or three prophets speak, and let the others judge. (1 Cor. 14:29)

Operation of the gifts requires cooperation from yielded Christians; however, human vessels do not become puppets, act unconsciously, or go into trances.

And the spirits of the prophets are subject to the prophets. (1 Cor. 14:32)

Believers actively cooperate with the Spirit. They participate intelligently and voluntarily. They are not in an ecstatic, euphoric stupor when the Spirit moves.

By faith and by an act of the will, Christians obey the Spirit's prompting to put themselves in positions where the Holy Spirit can use them and manifest Himself through them.

> *Present yourselves to God as being alive from the dead, and your*
> *members as instruments of righteousness to God.*   *(Rom. 6:13)*

It is time Christians begin to believe the Lord for more regular, normal manifestations of the gifts of the Spirit in the church. The Lord has purposed to work supernaturally through His supernatural people this way.

THE FEAR OF THE LORD

The disciples walked daily in the fear of God. Members of the church had seen a demonstration of what it meant to lie to the Holy Spirit. Frequent signs and wonders imposed an awesome reverence for God on the entire congregation. This fear "came upon every soul" *(Acts 2:43)*. The word *came* is in the imperfect tense and denotes a continual, abiding, long-lasting sense of awe.

Supernatural signs put the fear of the Lord not only on the New Testament church, but also on those outside the church. I. Howard Marshall comments, "the non-Christian population felt a certain apprehension over against a group in whose midst supernatural events were taking place."[28]

Luke refers to the the fear of the Lord in the New Testament church many times throughout Acts.

> *So great fear came upon all the church and upon all who heard*
> *these things.*   *(Acts 5:11)*

And walking in the fear of the Lord and in the comfort of the Holy Spirit, they were multiplied (Acts 9:31).

Fear fell on them all, and the name of the Lord Jesus was magnified. (Acts 19:17)

Fear can be healthy depending on the subject and the motivation for it. Fear keeps people from getting too close to the cliff's edge. It keeps them from sticking their hands in hot fire. It keeps them from becoming reckless. The fear of God brings positive benefits.

In the fear of the LORD there is strong confidence, and His children will have a place of refuge. The fear of the LORD is a fountain of life, to turn one away from the snares of death. (Prov. 14:26–27)

Oh, fear the LORD, you His saints! There is no want to those who fear Him. (Ps. 34:9)

The fear of God is an awesome reverence and respect toward God, knowing He is totally righteous and full of mercy and truth; He compensates and rewards the obedient in faith; and He judges, chastens, and punishes the disobedient in faith.

A person's fears become dominant in his life. The heart that fears the Lord is submitted to Him. The fear of the Lord shapes a God-centered way of life that acknowledges Him in all ways. A man who is aware of the presence of God and has a holy fear of Him allows no room for compromise or neutrality with sin and evil conduct.

The fear of the Lord is to hate evil; pride and arrogance and the evil way and the perverse mouth I hate. (Prov. 8:13)

A healthy fear keeps Christians from being self-assertive, proud, and boastful. It continually reminds them that they will give an account to God for their actions and words. Because of the fear of the Lord, they treat their fellow man decently. It restrains them from giving in to their base nature and keeps them from going to extremes.

Solomon was known as the wisest man on earth. At the end of his life his conclusion was: *"Fear God, and keep his commandments: for this is the whole duty of man"* (Eccl. 12:13). That summarized it for Solomon because he knew, *"God shall bring every work into judgment, with every secret thing, whether it be good, or whether it be evil"* (v. 14). In the end, every secret thing will be judged by a righteous God.

Believers need to be sure they fear God, not someone or something else. For instance, the Bible says not to fear false prophets *(Deut. 18:22)*, or the face of man *(Prov. 29:25)*, or man-made religions *(Isa. 29:13)*. Many who lead people astray use fear as one of their tools. They appeal to man's fears while pushing false doctrine, or they use fear of violence to dominate others' lives.

> *The fear of man brings a snare, but whoever trusts in the* Lord *shall be safe.* (Prov. 29:25)

All such fear is man-centered and self-centered, motivated by self-preservation and self-defense. The fear of the Lord is God-centered and motivated by true knowledge of Him, true love for Him, and commitment to do His will.

In a believer's desire to see the blessing of God and to see the promises of God fulfilled in his life, he must not be at the center of his own life, goals, and desires. When the focus of a Christian's faith and prayer is "God bless me, and give to me, and meet my needs, and be nice to me me me me me," then his primary concern is not for God's honor and glory but for his own benefit. To a degree he is not living in the fear of the Lord!

That does not mean God does not want to bless him. It means that only those who fear the Lord and put Him first really experience the blessing of the Lord. The local church needs to maintain essential teachings on the healthy fear of God.

As Charismatic-Pentecostal believers, we claim to want to rediscover the life and pattern of the New Testament church. But I am concerned about the absence of one of its most essential characteristics. The fear of God is lacking among us. We know the comfort of the Holy Spirit. We have learned to have liberty in the presence of the Lord. We have experienced the moving of the Holy Spirit and the joy He gives, but too often our motivation is to get whatever we can from the Lord when we are in His presence. This is a deficient attitude. It produces a careless lifestyle. Some call it "sloppy *agápe*."

THE BEGINNING OF WISDOM

A Gallup poll taken on religion in the United States found about fifty million Americans — almost one out of five — claimed to be "born again." It looked as if real revival was going on. But the answers to another poll question poured cold water on the initial impression. Pollsters asked, "Has your experience of being born again affected your lifestyle?" Only twelve percent said, "Yes." That meant eighty-eight percent of the people who claimed to be born again did not consider it relevant to their lifestyle. They had just added Jesus to their lives without letting Him make any practical difference at all.

That is not only tragic; it is frightening to think a man can claim to be born again without it affecting his lifestyle! The fear of the Lord will impact every aspect of a person's life. An ever-increasing wisdom will provide new insight into handling life's difficulties. And most of all, relationships with others will be conducted from God's point of view.

> *The fear of the LORD is the beginning of wisdom, and the knowledge of the Holy One is understanding.* (Prov. 9:10)

Where the entire community of believers is guided by the fear of God, people will be transformed and will show forth the love and glory of God. The power of God produces the glory of God. All onlookers will see a demonstration of God's nature in practical everyday living, and when Christians love one another, the world will believe. ✠

STUDY QUESTIONS

1. What is the significance of the phrase *signs and wonders*?

2. What is the role of the supernatural in the Christian church?

3. What was the attitude of the New Testament church toward the supernatural?

4. What is a miracle?

5. What is the significance of the power of the Holy Spirit in the church?

6. What is the purpose of miracles?

7. What is the role of the gifts of the Spirit in the supernatural presence of God in the church?

8. What is the fear of the Lord?

9. How did supernatural signs contribute to the fear of the Lord?

10. Why is the fear of the Lord an essential dynamic in the church?

8

Body Life

Now all who believed were together, and had all things in common, and sold their possessions and goods, and divided them among all, as anyone had need — *Acts 2:44–45*

OD WANTS TO REVEAL HIS GLORY IN THE CHURCH. GLORY is visible, so when God reveals it, people will see it. Glory is a manifestation of God's presence. The nation of Israel saw the glory of God several times. First, they saw it in the pillar of cloud in the wilderness. Next, God's glory rested on Mount Sinai as He spoke with Moses, and it looked like a consuming fire. The glory of the Lord also appeared at the dedications of the tabernacle built by Moses and the temple built by Solomon.

> *They looked toward the wilderness, and behold, the glory of the* LORD *appeared in the cloud.* *(Exod. 16:10; also see 24:16–18)*

> *Then the cloud covered the tabernacle of meeting, and the glory of the* LORD *filled the tabernacle.* *(Exod. 40:34; also see 1 Kings 8:10–11)*

> *Then the glory of the* LORD *appeared to all the people* *(Lev. 9:23)*

When Christ returns, people will "see the Son of Man coming in a cloud with power and great glory" *(Luke 21:27)*. However, before that happens, the glory of God will increase in the earth until the whole world is filled with the greatest demonstration of it, the Bible declares.

> *... but truly, as I live, all the earth shall be filled with the glory of the* LORD. (Num. 14:21)

> *The glory of the* LORD *shall be revealed, and all flesh shall see it together; for the mouth of the* LORD *has spoken.* (Isa. 40:5)

God will fill the earth with His glory by using His instrument in the earth today — the church. God's glory is an outward manifestation of His loving, self-sharing nature. When God's people take on godly character, His glory is revealed. Released in the church, the power and glory of God make the church conform more to the pattern — the image and likeness of God.

> *Unto Him be glory in the church.* (Eph. 3:21)

LIFE TOGETHER

The early church displayed the glory of God. His glory was revealed in transformed lives of early saints. *Acts* states, "All who believed were together." This cozy description of church life would be pretty comfortable if it ended here, but it continues. The first Christians also "had all things in common." That sounds strange, but it gets more offensive to the natural man. The text goes on to say that they "sold their possessions and goods, and divided them among all, as anyone had need."

The power of the Holy Spirit in the new birth produced such a radical transformation in these new believers that they wanted to share every aspect of their lives together. The greed and self-centeredness that had marked their lives of sin had been replaced by a holy, loving, self-sacrificing life together. It may sound like communism or at least communal living, but it was not.

Some commentaries state that in a few short years, Jerusalem would be downtrodden, and the believers would lose their material goods anyway. So the Holy Spirit prepared the church ahead of time, say the commentators. God just helped His disciples get rid of their money. These theologian writers wrongly conclude that this passage does not teach a principle or illustrate a dynamic in the New Testament church because it was just an isolated incident.

The Lord definitely did not teach communism and did not necessarily teach communal living. The text says believers went "from house to house" *(v. 46)*, so they must have had houses. They certainly did not sell everything they had; however, it appears they sold extra houses and lands and put the profits together to benefit the entire church community.

As Luke wrote *Acts*, he used language describing the ongoing lifestyle in the church. People who had repented, believed, and been baptized "were together," he states. *Were* is in the imperfect tense and could be translated "were continually together." *Together* is a unique expression used only by Luke and could be worded as "were continually added to them" or "were in fellowship with one another in unity of purpose and devotion."

Verse *44* states new believers "had all things in common." The imperfect tense for *had* means they were continually having. The word translated *common* is *koinós*, which means common, ordinary, or unhallowed. It is related to *koinōnía*, the Greek word for fellowship. F. F. Bruce comments, "with a deep sense of their unity in the Messiah, [they] gave up the idea of private property and 'had all things common.'" [29]

The experience of these early believers so changed them that instead of grabbing, they were giving. Instead of wanting something from God, they said, "Lord, what can we do for you? How can we bless? How can we be involved?" They demonstrated God's power and glory in their self-sacrificing ways. Their character confirmed their message. On the basis of these two witnesses — character and message — 3,000 converts were convinced of the genuineness of Jesus' Messiahship and were added to the church.

GIFTS REQUIRE LOVE

Character weaknesses in the disciples originally had hindered Christ's evangelistic work. Thousands of people had known about Him and had seen Him perform phenomenal miracles like cleansing lepers, casting out demons, opening blind eyes, and feeding the 5,000 with a few loaves and fishes. Five hundred had witnessed the ascension of Christ. His life marked a break from Old Testament times, in which only a few miracles took place — maybe one every fifty or 100 years. Yet, after all His miracles and ministry, He had only 120 hardcore disciples in the upper room who said, "We're followers of Jesus. He is the Messiah. He is the way, the truth and life. We're going to give our lives to Him and die for Him." One hundred and twenty!

Why were Jesus and his disciples not more effective in their ministry over three and one-half years? Jesus said to the crowd, "I have proved I am the Messiah by My works. Now, come and join My band of disciples." Why did more not come? What happened to the rest of the onlookers?

The lifestyle and character of the disciples contradicted Christ's message. Prior to the Day of Pentecost that band was selfish. The disciples were greedy. A thief was among their number. They were sectarian. When they saw someone else doing something in the name of Jesus, they ran over and said, "Lord, call down fire from heaven and burn them to a crisp." They were politically motivated. They always jockeyed for position. "Who is going to be the greatest?" they wondered. They were nationalistic. They did not really care for the Gentiles or the Samaritans. All they wanted to know was, "Are you going to set up the kingdom in Israel at this time? Who will have the lead positions? Who will sit right and left of your throne?" When children came, the disciples rebuked them. They had no time for the little people. "Get out of here, you brats!" they said. "This is the Messiah!" When a man sitting in rags said, "Help me Lord; help me," all they could say was, "Shut up dirty beggar. Don't you know who this is? You must have done something wrong or you wouldn't be in that mess." When the crowd was hungry, they advised Jesus, "Tell them to get out of here. We're not going to do anything about it." Jesus' signs and wonders had supported His message, but He could not be separated from His disciples.

Today men and women with character weaknesses and impure motives operate in the gifts and cause serious problems for the church. The problem is not with the gifts but with the people who use the gifts. The apostle Paul said, "I am nothing" *(1 Cor. 13:2)*. He did not say, "the gift is nothing."

When young, immature Christians see gifted ministers of the Gospel be immoral yet prophesy and get answers to prayer, they question, "Why, God?" Some observers tend to overreact and write off the gifts, but spiritual gifts are biblical and are needed in the church.

Signs, wonders, and miracles all demonstrate God's power, but His eternal purpose is to form the image of His Son in His people! He wants to release His love and reproduce His loving character in people who will release it to others! That will demonstrate God's glory in a way that will fill the earth. Jesus wants an intimate love relationship with people.

When the very gifted come before the Lord, they will say, "Lord, Lord, have we not prophesied in Your name, cast out demons in Your name, and done many wonders in Your name?" The Lord will say, "I never knew you" *(Matt. 7:22–23)*. The word *knew*, refers to the intimacy of a husband-wife relationship. In other words, He will say "I never had an intimate relationship with you."

Notice Jesus' full statement, "I never knew you; depart from Me, you who practice lawlessness." He did not say, "Let your gift depart from me." Lawless people are not in harmony with the Lord. They have no relationship with Him. Love does not motivate their activities.

The Bible does not say, "Now abide faith, hope and gifts, and the greatest of these is gifts." It actually says, *"Now abide faith, hope, love, these three; but the greatest of these is love" (1 Cor. 13:13)*. Love must motivate the gifts. Without love, the manifestation of gifts will be hollow, empty, and of no lasting value. They will not impart life or accomplish the will of God. They will be like sounding brass and tinkling cymbals. A man may have faith to move mountains and perform miracles, but without love, he is nothing (see *1 Cor. 13:2*).

The most common reason people give for rejecting the Gospel is hypocrisy in the church. A church without Christlike character may have evidence of the miraculous, and people will come; but not for long. The fruit will not remain. "That preacher has power," they will say, "But I don't like being with those people. They fight all the time."

Where people see an ongoing demonstration of the love of God, they notice something unusual — miraculous — has taken place.

IMBALANCES INHIBIT LIFE

I grew up in a Pentecostal environment. As a young man, I traveled as an evangelist. In 1951 my father pioneered a church and I worked with him. I became the senior pastor in 1959, and I have pastored the same church for my entire adult life.

I thank God for that heritage. I praise God for what I have been taught, no matter how many mistakes may have been made. I thank God for the leadership of our forefathers. I said that to say this: I have seen two things inhibit the release of the lifestyle God wants in the church. First, the deifying of ministry positions; second, the deifying of the gifts.

Ministry Deified Some say full-time ministry is the greatest vocation. They think there is no higher calling than apostles, prophets, evangelists, pastors, or teachers. They think church leadership is the so-called elite of the elite. Others may not verbalize it, but they imply the same thing.

Leaders themselves may think, "We are the leadership. We are the cream — the most valuable ones. We know we are the cream because cream comes to the top. We lead the church! You obey the leadership; you submit to the leadership; you listen to us because we have all the answers and will tell you what to do." Elders may even condescend to deacons and belittle their servant's role.

Ten percent of a congregation may serve in leadership. God puts people in those positions. He gives leaders to the church as gifts, but the remaining ninety percent is just as important. They are not second-class citizens.

Even laymen will say, "I really missed God. I should have gone to Bible School. I felt the call when I was a teenager and I did not go. I got married and had five kids, and now I'm only a plumber. I sure missed it." Did they miss it, or has the ministry been elevated out of balance? The professional clergy has been literally deified.

Gifts Deified Pentecostal and Charismatic churches tend to deify gifts of the Spirit and the people who manifest them in public worship services. The gifts must operate in the church, no question about it. But be realistic. Here again only ten percent of the people ever publicly minister a gift in the corporate gathering. Every Christian can and should be used by the Holy Spirit in his or her neighborhood or on the job, but in the congregation, maybe ten percent actually get up in front of the people, prophesy, give words of knowledge or wisdom, heal the sick, or work miracles.

If the operation of gifts in the public gathering is built up to be the most important thing, then most church members will be frustrated. In a church of 2,000, maybe 200 will minister a spiritual gift during the year. Deification of the public manifestation of spiritual gifts leaves most people unfulfilled. They feel they have no part to play in the release of God's glory in and through the church.

Some Christians think that gatherings other than corporate church services are not important because if they give a word, only a few people will hear and applaud. If they pray for the sick, no one sees and applauds. "Go to my neighbor and visit the sick?" they ask. "I like to get up where everyone can see the power demonstrated and see the healing."

The corporate gathering is an important part of the house of God. It is a wonderful place to minister healing and be healed, but believers must not deify elements of the corporate gathering, church leaders and the public manifestation of the gifts. If they do, the church will be like an eight-cylinder engine running on one cylinder.

If ten percent can release the power of God, what could the other ninety percent do?

THE BODY OF CHRIST

One of the most powerful, profound pictures the New Testament gives of the church is as the body of Christ. As a body, the church is made up of interconnected members.

> *For as we have many members in one body, but all the members do not have the same function, so we, being many, are one body in Christ, and individually members of one another.* (Rom. 12:4–5)

- The body of Christ has many members.

> *But now indeed there are many members, yet one body.*
> (1 Cor. 12:20)

- Each member is connected to each other.

For by one Spirit we were all baptized into one body —
whether Jews or Greeks, whether slaves or free — and
have all been made to drink into one Spirit.   *(1 Cor. 12:13)*

- Each member depends on the other members.

And the eye cannot say to the hand, "I have no need of
you;" nor again the head to the feet, "I have no need of
you." No, much rather, those members of the body which
seem to be weaker are necessary.   *(1 Cor. 12:21–22)*

- Each member has an important place and function in the body.

Now you are the body of Christ, and members individu-
ally.   *(1 Cor. 12:27)*

The body of Christ is visible. God is invisible *(1 Tim. 1:17)*. Therefore, the entire body of Christ — not just the specially gifted ten percent — can show forth the glory of God to the surrounding community and the world.

THE MANDATE TO SERVE

God has put every person in this life for one main purpose: to express His love in the midst of a loveless, selfish world. The love of God is expressed through serving. THE HIGHEST THING ANY CHRISTIAN CAN POSSIBLY DO IS TO SERVE.

The spirit of servanthood penetrated the New Testament church. All 3,120 were trained to serve. The believers had miracles in their midst, and when spiritual gifts, healings, and miracles were needed, then the church believed God to provide them. However, other times required other expressions. Practical expressions of love demonstrate pure and perfect religion. James gave early believers two practical expressions:

> *Pure and undefiled religion before God and the Father is this: to visit orphans and widows in their trouble, and to keep oneself unspotted from the world.* (James 1:27)

A saint does great things when he serves, letting the love of God flow through him in whatever way might be needed. Nothing is greater in God's kingdom.

Ninety percent of all church members may never publicly manifest a spiritual gift. Many are not skilled in public speaking. Many are not highly educated but are hard working and love God. Many are shy and introverted and will not have a public ministry. If they knew that serving the widow, the fatherless, and the aged was spiritual, they would be motivated. Ninety percent of the body would get off the sidelines and begin to minister the way God has ordained. Leaders must convince the saints that they *are* in the ministry.

Jesus said:

> *When the Son of Man comes in His glory, and all the holy angels with him, then He will sit on the throne of His glory. Then the King will say to those on His right hand, "Come, you blessed of my Father, inherit the kingdom prepared for you from the foundation of the world."* (Matt. 25:31, 34)

Why? Because they healed the sick or prophesied? No!

> *... for I was hungry and you gave Me food; I was thirsty and you gave Me drink; I was a stranger and you took Me in; I was naked and you clothed Me; I was sick and you visited Me; I was in prison*

and you came to Me ... Assuredly, I say to you, inasmuch as you
did it to one of the least of these My brethren, you did it to Me.
(Matt. 25:35, 36, 40)

Every believer encounters sick people and should be willing to pray for them even if he is not specifically anointed with a gift of healing. Just visiting sick, needy, or old folks is a spiritual ministry. Being an encouragement, serving, and caring for others in practical ways is just as much an expression of the love, power, and glory of God as being able to supernaturally raise them from a sickbed.

When believers see the hungry, they might not break bread and feed the multitude supernaturally, but feeding the hungry in any way is spiritual work. Under God's plan, every church member is released and fulfilled, and every local church is fully mobilized.

A Christian has to begin serving before God will confirm his ministry. Sitting at home, reading the paper, or watching the evening news, I have never led one person to the Lord, seen one miracle, or had one answer to prayer. However, when I go see someone in the hospital — even when I am tired — the Lord moves through my availability. I have to discipline myself to get up and drive to the hospital to be in a position to bless others. Then, even if the person I came to see does not seem to need me, the lady in the bed across the room may say, "Pastor, before you go will you pray for me?"

CHANGED HEARTS

Believers filled with the Holy Spirit on the Day of Pentecost received *dúnamis* — power — dynamite. But what did they do with it? Blow up the place? One translation puts *Acts 1:8* as follows: *"After that the Holy Ghost comes upon you, you shall receive ability."* Ability for what? To do whatever needs to be done in the name of the Lord.

The power of the Holy Spirit was the only difference in them after the Day of Pentecost. It gave them a spirit of love, caring, and giving.

They spoke in tongues, and the supernatural was open to them, but the greatest miracle of all was that their hearts had been transformed. If their hearts had not been changed, then the gifts would not have been effective and their ministry would have failed.

A Christian cannot reach into people's hearts unless his heart has been changed, and the purpose of the fullness of the Holy Spirit is to change hearts.

How much is serving emphasized in the church today? How much recognition goes to the usher, the custodian, the Sunday school teacher, and others who pour out their lives week after week? Comments like, "He's just a deacon, just an usher, just a custodian" can kill initiative to serve in the house of the Lord.

Usually, people who want to be "in the ministry" think they need to be exalted and stand on the platform behind the microphone. They think servants are unspiritual and unable to make a difference. The same thoughts ran through the minds of James and John. Before they were filled with the Holy Spirit, they asked for permission to sit on the right and left of Jesus' throne in His kingdom. Jesus told them, *"to sit on My right hand and on My left is not Mine to give; but it is for those for whom it is prepared" (Mark 10:40).* They were not the only disciples who wanted to be exalted. The next verse says, *"when the ten heard it, they began to be greatly displeased."* They all wanted positions next to Jesus and knew they had only two available spots to fight over. James and John merely got to Jesus first.

Jesus said, "You don't know what spirit you are of. If you live according to Gentile rules, you will lord over people. That is the way the world thinks." Christians do not have to worry about recognition in the kingdom of God. The Lord will take care of recognizing people who respond properly to His Lordship and serve others with pure hearts.

Jesus revealed the way to true greatness:

Yet it shall not be so among you; but whoever desires to become great among you shall be your servant. (Mark 10:43)

Greatness lies in servanthood. Next, He said:

And whoever of you desires to be first shall be slave of all. (Mark 10:44)

It is a paradox. To get to the highest place, a believer must take the lowest position. When Christians stand before the Lord on judgment day, they will be rewarded for faithfully and wholeheartedly doing what God told them to do. Equal rewards will go to all who gave their time, money, and lives to serve others. They will not be rewarded because they were pastors or apostles.

In Jerusalem, Peter preached to many people who had heard Jesus speak and had seen him perform miracles. Peter told them that if they would repent, be baptized and filled with the Spirit, their hearts would be changed. They would be translated out of the kingdom of darkness into the kingdom of the Son of God. He said that the Spirit would empower them to love as they had never loved before and care for people as they had never cared before.

They had been 3,000 typical Jewish believers under a law they were unable to keep. They believed the Gospel and came to Christ. They had been under the old covenant but knew the Lord had promised to make a new covenant.

I will put my law in their minds, and write it on their hearts. (Jer. 31:33)

With the law in their hearts, people do not have to live under the constant pressure of trying to obey the commandments by will power alone.

Imagine what the neighbors of these Jerusalem Christians thought. Maybe they had been competitors always trying to keep up with the Jonesteins. When one neighbor got a new chariot, the other bought one too. When one bought new furniture, so did the other. Both families had the spirit of this world, thinking, "What can I get out of life? How can I get a promotion? How can I get bigger and better things?"

Suddenly, one looks across the street and notices differences. The Christian family does not do the same old things. Dad spends more time with the family. All of them go to worship together every week. Strangers show up at their house and stay all evening. They seem to be genuinely happy! The neighbors say, "Have you seen what following Christ has done in that home? Have you seen what it has done in the children? Have you seen how it affects their attitudes? These people are different!"

Dwight L. Moody said, "The world has not seen what God will do through one man who is totally yielded to God." And then he said, "I am determined to be that man." Moody's ministry shook the earth.

The true power in the church never has been released. The world has not yet seen what God can do through one local church or one generation totally yielded to God. Such a church will have unbelievable power — prayer power, serving power, loving power, caring power, and miraculous power. The basis and purpose of such power is to be a loving, selflessly serving community. The congregation must be released to be the kingdom community God designed it to be.

CARING FOR ONE ANOTHER

Sharing life with one another was not an abstract ideal for the New Testament church. The first Christians "put their money where their mouth was." They sold property and possessions to meet needs of others in the church. They had no covetousness or greed. A spirit of liberality prevailed.

To make sure no one needed food or shelter, believers with extra land and personal property, sold it and brought the money to the church elders for distribution. The text does not imply that they sold homes they needed to live in.

The word translated need means what is necessary for life or things a person is unable to do without. Some church members had ongoing needs (imperfect tense) that could be met no other way. The word *sold (Acts 2:45)* is in the imperfect tense, meaning that the believers were continually selling. They agreed to sell possessions as an ongoing solution to ongoing needs in the Christian community. They were continually *dividing* or distributing (imperfect tense) their goods according to the actual needs of their brothers and sisters.

Paul called this "equality."

For I do not mean that others should be eased and you burdened; but by an equality, that now at this time your abundance may supply their lack, that their abundance also may supply your lack- that there may be equality. (2 Cor. 8:13–14)

New Testament books abound with examples of giving "to the necessities of the saints." Some churches, like the one at Philippi, often gave beyond what the congregation could afford. All the churches had constant concern for the poor, the widow, and disaster victims.

... distributing to the needs of the saints, given to hospitality. (Rom. 12:13)

And with great power the apostles gave witness to the resurrection of the Lord Jesus. And great grace was upon them all. Nor was there anyone among them who lacked; for all who were posses-

sors of lands or houses sold them, and brought the proceeds of the things that were sold, and laid them at the apostles' feet; and they distributed to each as anyone had need. (Acts 4:33–35)

Then one of them, named Agabus, stood up and showed by the Spirit that there was going to be a great famine throughout all the world, which also happened in the days of Claudius Caesar. Then the disciples, each according to his ability, determined to send relief to the brethren dwelling in Judea (Acts 11:28–29).

The Scriptures endorse concern for the poor and needy.

Blessed is he who considers the poor; the LORD will deliver him in time of trouble. (Ps. 41:1)

He who has pity on the poor lends to the LORD, and He will pay back what he has given. (Prov. 19:17)

Whoever shuts his ears to the cry of the poor will also cry himself and not be heard. (Prov. 21:13)

He who gives to the poor will not lack, but he who hides his eyes will have many curses. (Prov. 28:27)

The righteous considers the cause of the poor, but the wicked does not understand such knowledge. (Prov. 29:7)

The poor and suffering are close to the heart of God. Helping the needy, serving, caring, sharing, and visiting is lending to the Lord, and the Lord repays His loans *(Prov. 19:17)*. The motivation for works must be compassion, not self-righteous ego. The entire congregation must have the same motivation.

Sodom was destroyed primarily for neglecting the poor and needy, not for immorality.

> *Look, this was the iniquity of your sister Sodom: She and her daughter had pride, fullness of food, and abundance of idleness; neither did she strengthen the hand of the poor and needy.*
>
> *(Ezek. 16:49)*

The local church built according to the New Testament pattern takes care of its own hurting members. Members should not have to seek assistance and security elsewhere. A church is out of balance if it says "God bless you," but does not meet the needs of the hurting.

> *If a brother or sister is naked and destitute of daily food, and one of you says to them, 'Depart in peace, be warmed and filled,' but you do not give them the things which are needed for the body, what does it profit? Thus also faith by itself, if it does not have works, is dead.*
>
> *(James 2:15–17)*

The dynamics of the early church touched the believers' lifestyles in a way that seems foreign to the twentieth-century church. However, restoration will take place in the latter days prior to the second corning of Christ. The church that sees Christ's return will have a double portion of all the dynamics of the early church. It will have people who are selfless, loving, giving, and serving. ✠

STUDY QUESTIONS

1. What is the glory of God? How is it revealed in the church?

2. What is the first result of the fear of God?

3. How does love demonstrate the power of God?

4. Why is deifying the ministry a problem?

5. Why is deifying the gifts of the Spirit a problem?

6. In what way is the church the body of Christ?

7. What is the highest mandate in the kingdom of God?

8. Who is truly great in the kingdom of God?

9. What will be the basis for our reward on the day of judgment?

10. How did members of the Jerusalem church demonstrate love for one another?

9 Assembling Together

*And they, continuing daily with one accord in
the temple, and breaking bread from house
to house, did eat their meat with gladness
and singleness of heart.*   — Acts 2:46

ELIEVERS IN THE JERUSALEM CHURCH SERVED ONE
another selflessly as they spent time together. Covenant relationships required quantity and quality time to maintain, both
of which were given willingly. Church was not a place to go to on
Sunday morning to fulfill a religious duty. It was their community.[30]
It involved all aspects of life every day.

Day to day, the disciples devoted themselves to being together.
Verse *46* uses the same strong word continuing that began verse *42*.
They continually adhered to and dedicated themselves to a life
together. That meant they were together at the same time, in the
same place.

The Greek word translated *church* is *ekklēsía*. It comes from
two words: *ek,* which means "out of", and *klēsis,* which means "a
calling". It refers to people called to an assembly. It does not refer to
a building but to a particular group of people assembled for a particular purpose. It is the assembly of the saints.

Among the Greeks, it referred to a body of citizens gathered
to discuss the affairs of state. In the Greek translation of the Old
Testament, it designated the gathering of Israel, summoned for any

definite purpose, or a gathering regarded as representative of the whole nation. No wonder the apostles so strongly urged believers to assemble together.

And being assembled together with them, He commanded. (Acts 1:4)

The place where they were assembled together was shaken.(Acts 4:31)

The strongest exhortation comes from the writer of the book of Hebrews. He called the saints to persevere in difficult, discouraging times and to keep getting together to encourage one another.

Not forsaking the assembling of ourselves together, as is the manner of some, but exhorting one another, and so much the more as you see the Day approaching. (Heb. 10:25)

Consider the way other translations phrase this verse:

Not forsaking or neglecting to assemble together [as believers], as is the habit of some people, but admonishing-warning, urging and encouraging-one another, and all the more faithfully as you see the day approaching. (Amplified)[31]

Not abandoning ... our common assembly. (Knox)[32]

Not neglecting our own church meeting. (Barclay)[33]

Not staying away from our meetings. (New English Bible)[34]

And let us not hold aloof from our church meetings. (Phillips)[35]

The New Testament church commonly gathered weekly to celebrate Jesus' resurrection on the first day of the week. Every Sunday was Easter for them.

Now on the first day of the week, when the disciples came together to break bread, Paul, ready to depart the next day, spoke to them and continued his message until midnight. (Acts 20:7)

In the name of our Lord Jesus Christ, when you are gathered together, along with my spirit, with the power of our Lord Jesus Christ. (1 Cor. 5:4; see also 11:18, 33)

How is it then, brethren? Whenever you come together, each of you has a psalm ... (1 Cor. 14:26)

On the first day of the week let each one of you lay something aside, storing up as he may prosper. (1 Cor. 16:2)

UNITY AND DIVERSITY

The New Testament church gathered together in one accord, literally meaning with one mind, one spirit, or one passion. The same expression appears twelve times in the New Testament, eleven in the book of *Acts*. Whether it was to pray, to discuss problems, or to respond to preaching, the New Testament church came together with one accord.

These all continued with one accord in prayer and supplication. (Acts 1:14)

So when they heard that, they raised their voice to God with one accord. (Acts 4:24; see also v. 32)

And they were all with one accord in Solomon's Porch. (Acts 5:12)

It seemed good to us, being assembled with one accord, to send chosen men to you with our beloved Barnabas and Paul. (Acts 15:25)

Jesus taught that a house divided against itself cannot stand *(Matt. 12:25).* To last, a house must have unity. The church is a unified organism, a living, harmonious whole. God designed it to function with one mind.

Be of the same mind toward one another. Do not set your mind on high things, but associate with the humble. Do not be wise in your own opinion. (Rom. 12:16)

Be of good comfort, be of one mind, live in peace; and the God of love and peace will be with you. (2 Cor. 13:11)

Fulfill my joy by being like-minded, having the same love, being of one accord, of one mind. (Phil. 2:2)

This is not a mechanical unity but a unity of the Spirit, rising from people's hearts. It is a unity made possible by the fact that all the members of the body are born again by the Spirit. They are "one" because they are all of one Spirit "endeavoring to keep the unity of the Spirit in the bond of peace" *(Eph. 4:3).*

This essential level of unity forms the basis for an overall expression of unity. If Christians work to maintain their unity, it grows into practical harmony in the body. Unity of the Spirit was to lead to unity of the faith.

... till we all come to the unity of the faith and of the knowledge of the Son of God, to a perfect man, to the measure of the stature of the fullness of Christ. (Eph. 4:13)

*Now I plead with you, brethren, by the name of our Lord Jesus
Christ, that you all speak the same thing, and that there be no
divisions among you, but that you be perfectly joined together in
the same mind and in the same judgment.*　　　(1 Cor. 1:10)

Unity is one of the most powerful forces on the earth. People of
one mind cannot be stopped. They can achieve almost anything they
purpose to do.

*Indeed the people are one and they all have one language, and this
is what they begin to do; now nothing that they propose to do will
be withheld from them.*　　　(Gen. 11:6)

The greatest enemy of the church is division. Sin and self-centeredness divide the members of the body of Christ making them
weak and ineffective.

*Now I urge you, brethren, note those who cause divisions and
offenses, contrary to the doctrine which you learned, and
avoid them.*　　　(Rom. 16:17)

*You arc still carnal. For where there are envy, strife, and divisions
among you, arc you not carnal and behaving like mere men?*
　　　(1 Cor. 3:3).

*These arc sensual persons, who cause divisions, not having
the Spirit.*　　　(Jude 19)

The blessing of the Lord rests on people who have one heart and
mind together. The life of God flows without hindrance between
members of the body of Christ when it has no divisions. Unity also
enables God's life to flow to those outside of the body.

*Behold, how good and how pleasant it is for brethren to dwell
together in unity! It is like the precious oil upon the head, running
down on the beard, the beard of Aaron, running down on the edge
of his garments. It is like the dew of Hermon, descending upon the
mountains of Zion; for there the LORD commanded the blessing —
life forevermore.*   *(Ps. 133)*

God displayed His power in unified assemblies of His people at:

- **The Tabernacle of Moses.** *"On the first day of the first month
  you shall set up the tabernacle of the tent of meeting. ... Then the
  cloud covered the tabernacle of meeting, and the glory of the LORD
  filled the tabernacle."*   *(Exod. 40:2, 34)*

- **The Temple of Solomon.** *"Indeed it came to pass, when the
  trumpeters and singers were as one, to make one sound to be heard
  in praising and thanking the LORD, and when they lifted up their
  voice with the trumpets and cymbals and instruments of music,
  and praised the LORD, saying: 'For He is good, for His mercy
  endures forever,' that the house, the house of the LORD, was filled
  with a cloud, so that the priests could not continue ministering
  because of the cloud; for the glory of the LORD filled the house
  of God."*   *(2 Chron. 5:13–14)*

- **The Day of Pentecost.** *"Now when the Day of Pentecost had
  fully come, they were all with one accord in one place. And suddenly there came a sound from heaven, as of a rushing mighty
  wind, and it filled the whole house where they were sitting.
  Then there appeared to them divided tongues, as of fire, and one
  sat upon each of them. And they were all filled with the Holy
  Spirit and began to speak with other tongues, as the Spirit gave
  them utterance."*   *(Acts 2:1–4)*

Christians know they are dwelling in unity when they are sensitive to their brother's and sister's needs. When my toes are stepped on, my whole body feels the pain. Likewise, when something happens to another member of the body, everyone in unity is affected. If individuals cannot feel the hurts of the wounded or rejoice in the successes of others in a local church, they lack unity.

And if one member suffers, all the members suffer with it; or if one member is honored, all the members rejoice with it.   *(1 Cor. 12:26)*

Humility lays the groundwork for unity. Pride separates people. Diotrephes separated his church from the apostle John and excommunicated members who would not cooperate because he "loved to be first" *(3 John 9)*. A servant's humble heart filled with God's love and energized by His Spirit makes unity possible.

At times church members may disagree on doctrines and methods. The apostolic church certainly had disagreements, but true unity means the saints work it out. The beloved brothers and sisters are committed to working through problems without becoming divided.

Paul exhorted Christians to "endeavor to keep the unity of the Spirit." *Endeavor* means to use speed, make effort, or to be prompt or earnest. *Keep* means to fix your eye on an object like a sentry standing guard on the perimeter of a military camp. People must work at unity. It is worth the effort.

Any time tragedy strikes the church, disagreement arises over policy, or the church faces a strategic time of decision, all members must rally to the common cause of maintaining unity in the body.

The church is a multi-membered, diverse organism. Each member has a unique, individual function and significance. At the same time, each member's role relates to the purpose of the entire body.

> *But one and the same Spirit works all these things, distributing to each one individually as He wills. For as the body is one and has many members, but all the members of that one body, being many, are one body, so also is Christ.* (1 Cor. 12:11–12)

No single member of the body is more important than another. In fact, each member gains its significance by belonging to the whole. When each member has equal respect and care for the others, unity is maintained.

> *For in fact the body is not one member but many. If the foot should say, 'Because I am not a hand, I am not of the body,' is it therefore not of the body? And if the ear should say, 'Because I am not an eye, I am not of the body,' is it therefore not of the body? If the whole body were an eye, where would be the hearing? If the whole were hearing, where would be the smelling? But now God has set the members, each one of them, in the body just as He pleased.* (1 Cor. 12:14–18)

Without individual members, a body cannot exist. It could not function and bear fruit unless each member was different. People tend to reject others who are dissimilar, yet all are absolutely necessary to have a healthy body. When everyone sees the reality of the multi-membered body, the church will have unity with diversity.

> *And if they were all one member, where would the body be? But now indeed there are many members, yet one body. And the eye cannot say to the hand, "I have no need of you"; nor again the head to the feet, "I have no need of you." No, much rather, those members of the body which seem to be weaker are necessary.* (1 Cor. 12:19–22)

God desires that different ministries function together at the same time. Diverse needs among the sheep require diverse shepherding skills. It is the only way pastoral leadership can hope to meet all the needs. God's plan calls for unity of fellowship among diverse ministers and members. That approach brings abundant life and health to the house of God.

The principle of unity and diversity transformed my outlook on church life, my attitude to fellow ministers, and my relationship to other church members. No matter how different we are, we need each other. I actually need people who are different from me to help me effectively minister to the church.

The church needs the ministry of the pastor, but it also needs the ministry of the prophet, the evangelist, some good teachers, administrators, fatherly apostles, helpers, and others. Rather than weakening a church, diverse ministry gives it strength. Just like the diverse members of a physical body, all members of Christ's body work together to perform a wide range of tasks.

Many church fights could be avoided; a lot of schisms could be mended, and splinter groups would not have to stray onto tangents if they would see the importance of maintaining unity with diversity. The local church is a lot healthier and more effective when differing ministries are allowed to exist side-by-side.

CELL AND CELEBRATION

New Testament believers met in mass at the temple and in small cell groups at family homes. The word translated temple refers to the entire temple complex. One specific reference, *Acts 3:1–2*, records Peter and John going to the Beautiful gate at the ninth hour, the "hour of prayer", and verse *11* refers to their gathering at Solomon's Porch. (See also *John 10:23; Acts 5:12*.)

In the four porticos of the temple, scribes conducted schools and held debates while merchants set up stalls for business. Solomon's

Colonnade or Porch ran along the east side of the temple over-looking the Kidron Valley. The porch was forty-nine feet long and had two rows of columns. According to the historian Josephus, the porch had a covered area supported by a platform. Several thousand people could have met there easily.

At the temple in one group, the congregation celebrated in worship with a special dynamic. They preached the Gospel to whoever may have been looking on. All members received instruction from the apostles at the same time. It promoted unity and helped them speak with one voice.

House-to-house meetings brought believers together to break bread in small groups in neighborhoods throughout the city. *Breaking bread* is the same phrase used in verse *42* to refer to worship. Church historians say many homes had worship rooms where Christians met.[36] In addition to worship, the cell also provided a place where each individual contributed something from the Lord — prayer, personal ministry, fellowship or mutual encouragement. The believers did not cease in these things.

And daily in the temple, and in every house, they did not cease teaching and preaching Jesus as the Christ (Acts 5:42).[37]

CELEBRATION	CELL
Corporate Worship	Fellowship
Gospel Preaching	Body Ministry
Pastoral Instruction	Pastoral Care
Community Witness	Personal Witness

The home fellowship meeting is one of the great blessings of today and is important to the growth of the church. Some say the largest group a person can relate to meaningfully is 200, and the largest group that allows close personal relationships is twelve to twenty persons. Congregational gatherings have a dynamic that cannot be found in the home setting, but everyone in the church needs a small group of close relationships. Everyone needs a place and time to open his heart one-to-one or in a small group and to share his thoughts and needs with others.[38]

I love the corporate gathering of the saints, so I was dismayed at a trend in the early 1980s to reduce the number of congregational services to make room for more home or cell meetings. God was speaking to the church in those days about reviving home meetings, but some swung the pendulum too far. Nothing takes the place of the corporate gathering of the body of Jesus.

The pendulum can swing too far the other way, too. Believers can say the Sunday morning congregational meeting is the most important thing in Christianity. They can claim what they received last Sunday will last all week and they do not need to fill up again until next Sunday.

Today the Lord is forming small groups in the church to prepare for the great harvest of the last days. When harvest sends membership into the thousands, the local church will have the strength of large numbers plus the warmth of small groups. A megachurch can follow the New Testament pattern if it maintains strong small groups. It must have both the in-the-temple and the house-to-house dimensions of body life.

Old Testament Israel followed this pattern as well. The camp of Israel may have had two to three million people in it, but they were divided into groups of one thousand, one hundred, fifty, and ten. Levels of fellowship, care, ministry, and authority made it resemble a megachurch with all the dynamics of large and small groups of various sizes.

Moreover you shall select from all the people able men, such as fear God, men of truth, hating covetousness; and place such over them to be rulers of thousands, rulers of hundreds, rulers of fifties, and rulers of tens (Exod. 18:21).

When Jesus ministered to large numbers of people, He divided them into small groups before proceeding.

There were about five thousand men. And He said to His disciples, "Make them sit down in groups of fifty." (Luke 9:14)

For true spiritual growth to occur, each member must minister to others and receive ministry from others. Every part must supply something to the whole. Only then will the body enjoy health and grow.

... speaking the truth in love, may grow up in all things into Him who is the head — Christ — from whom the whole body, joined and knit together by what every joint supplies, according to the effective working by which every part does its share, causes growth of the body for the edifying of itself in love. (Eph. 4:15–16)

The Lord does not add members to the body just to make it larger. Each member makes unique contributions to the unique mission of that body in that community and that generation. Small groups provide opportunities for more people to contribute. Growth occurs in the congregational gathering, but small groups stimulate spiritual life and bring people to maturity faster. They breed relationships that hold people accountable to each other. Accountability strengthens disciple-making programs.

Pastoral care also is most effective in small groups because staying informed and sensitive to needs of individuals and families is easier. A pastor of a small group who keeps in touch with the group's members can care for people more consistently.

A kingdom community has large and small group emphases. Both are absolutely necessary! A return to the simple but effective New Testament pattern brings rich results.

THE JOY OF HOSPITALITY

Early believers practiced hospitality which is still a virtue. Christian homes are to be open as places to gather and share from the heart. The word translated hospitality in the New Testament simply means love of strangers. It is a practical, demonstrable love of people, especially for those unloved by others.

> *... distributing to the needs of the saints, given to hospitality.*
>
> *(Rom. 12:13).*

Middle eastern culture highly valued hospitality. Abraham, the father of the faithful, showed one of the best examples of giving love in a practical way. He entertained three visitors and discovered One was really the Lord and two were angels.

> *Do not forget to entertain strangers, for by so doing some have unwittingly entertained angels.* *(Heb. 13:2)*

The Jerusalem church was not just a crowd or a central gathering place. Believers went from house to house, sharing their lives, eating at one another's table, praying together, allowing the Holy Spirit to breathe upon them in small groups. They had enthusiasm for life, abounding joy, and rejoicing hearts.

The word *gladness* hardly does the Greek word justice. It means exaltation and extreme joy. It conveys the angel's words to Zacharias informing him that he would have "*joy and gladness, and many will rejoice at his* [John's] *birth"* *(Luke 1:14)*. Elizabeth used it when *"the babe* [John] *leaped in my womb for joy"* at the arrival of Mary, pregnant with the Messiah *(Luke 1:44)*. A form of this word is also used in Mary's Magnificat: *"My soul magnifies the Lord, and my spirit has rejoiced in God my Savior"* *(Luke 1:46)*. It was also said that Christ was anointed with "the oil of gladness," extreme joy, above His fellows *(Heb. 1:9; see also Jude 24)*.

Unquenchable joy continually filled the homes of the disciples and enveloped their daily lives. Exuberant joy marked the presence of God in their midst. Ongoing joy like this cannot be manufactured. It is an inner contentment independent of circumstances and based on a vital relationship with the Lord. The Christian alive with the Spirit of Christ can carry on life's tasks, face circumstances and adversity, and still have a deep-seated joy and peaceful rest.

Satan tries to destroy joy in the believer and in the local church. He attempts to kill the enthusiasm and excitement of being in the presence of God. When joy disappears, fruit withers *(Joel 1:9–12)* and strength shrinks *(Neh. 8:10)*. Israelites perished because they did not serve the Lord with gladness and a joyful heart *(Deut. 28:47)*.

Young people desperately crave joy. Youths who join cults frequently mention the loss of vibrant life in their churches as a reason for joining cults. At first, the cults seem to have more joyous spontaneity, life, excitement, and happiness. Later on, they prove to be superficial, phony coverups for various types of slavery.

Joy is infectious. It is appealing. It draws people to Christ. It is essential in Christian churches and homes. *"In Your presence is fullness of joy"* *(Ps. 16:11)*. Believers should pray with David: *"Restore to me the joy of Your salvation"* *(Ps. 51:12)*.

New Testament gatherings were known for "singleness of heart." This phrase means simple or sincere. This expression occurs only here and refers to a road that is smooth, free from rocks, so the traveler will not stumble or stub his toe. Vine defines it as "an unalloyed benevolence expressed in act."[39] Simplicity and sensitivity marked the fellowship and hospitality of these believers. They were committed to blessing each other. They were not motivated by self-centeredness or guile but helped each other along the pathway of life. They really loved one another.

> *By this all will know that you are My disciples, if you have love for one another.*   *(John 13:35)*

> *... that they all may be one, as You, Father, are in Me, and I in You; that they also may be one in Us, that the world may believe that You sent Me.*   *(John 17:21)*

Simple, sincere love built up the church and proved to onlookers that the grace of God had worked miracles in people. Their unity showed forth the glory of God to a divided, lonely people. Their love for one another proved that Jesus of Nazareth was the Lord of life and that his Gospel was Good News indeed.   ✠

STUDY QUESTIONS

1. What does the word translated *church* in the New Testament really mean?

2. What was the New Testament church's practice of assembling together?

3. What does *one accord* mean? How was it an aspect of the church?

4. What kind of unity is the church called to?

5. What is the greatest enemy of the church?

6. How is diversity made possible by unity?

7. What are the benefits of a gathering in the temple'?

8. What are the benefits of *house-to-house* gatherings?

9. How can spiritual growth be encouraged by house-to-house gatherings?

10. What role does the joy of the Lord play in this dynamic?

10

> ... *praising God, and having favor with all the people. And the Lord added to the church daily those who were being saved* — Acts 2:47

JUST AS JESUS "INCREASED IN FAVOR WITH GOD AND MAN" *(Luke 2:52)*, so also His early church won people's favor. Common citizens of the city noticed changes in Jesus' followers. Ordinary people with ordinary problems had been energized with life and power. They were no longer just human. Relationship with the Father had lifted them above their own limitations and made them avenues of His love to others.

God gives Christians favor in the eyes of unbelievers to influence them and shine light into their darkness. The word translated *favor* or *grace* is *cháris*. It refers to something that gives joy, pleasure, delight, or goodwill. It means lovingkindness that gives a recipient something he does not deserve. Grace flowed to all the believers and gave them favor in the eyes of others.[40] J. B. Phillips translates verse 47: *"They praised God continually and all the people respected them."*[41]

UPHOLD INTEGRITY

God and man favor the church when it adheres to a clear line of integrity. Believers who live uprightly obtain a good standing in the community. They command attention when they speak about the Gospel of Christ. Their pure, unspotted standards present a clear contrast to abnormal systems of the world.

Upright men and women have great potential to influence others. Noah found grace or favor in the eyes of the Lord, and human life was preserved from annihilation. Cornelius had an impeccable lifestyle and was instrumental in opening the door of salvation to the Gentiles. Note the following:

Now God had brought Daniel into the favor and goodwill of the chief of the eunuchs. (Dan. 1:9)

Let not mercy and truth forsake you; bind them around your neck, write them on the tablet of your heart, and so find favor and high esteem in the sight of God and man. (Prov. 3:3–4)

He who earnestly seeks good finds favor, but trouble will come to him who seeks evil. (Prov. 11:27)

A good man obtains favor from the LORD, *but a man of wicked intentions He will condemn.* (Prov. 12:2)

Fools mock at sin, but among the upright there is favor.
(Prov. 14:9; see also Prov. 14:35; 16:7)

No one respects a compromiser. A lukewarm church does not deserve favor. Its conduct brings reproach upon the Gospel and the name of Christ.

To change the destiny of cities, Christians need to gain the attention of people. They must command respect in the community. They find favor by upholding their integrity and righteousness in everyday living. Preaching doctrine is not an end in itself. Doctrines are to be applied to real-life situations. The church must make its conduct match its teaching.

Timothy ... will remind you of my way of life in Christ Jesus,
which agrees with what I teach everywhere in every church.

(1 Cor. 4:17 NIV)

LIGHT AND LEAVEN

Jesus is the Light of the world shining the light of God on all mankind. He shines on the saints because He wants them to walk in the light.

I am the light of the world. He who follows Me shall not walk in
darkness, but have the light of life. *(John 8:12)*

As believers walk in the light they shine like light for people walking in darkness. Jesus has called all who walk with Him to also be the light of the world.

You are the light of the world. A city that is set on a hill cannot be
hidden. Nor do they light a lamp and put it under a basket, but on
a lampstand, and it gives light to all who are in the house. Let your
light so shine before men, that they may see your good works and
glorify your Father in heaven. *(Matt. 5:14–16)*

As citizens in God's kingdom, the saints are like leaven in the midst of the world.

The kingdom of heaven is like leaven, which a woman took and
hid in three measures of meal till it was all leavened. *(Matt. 13:33)*

Christians have been mixed into the dough of the world by the King to infiltrate the whole loaf of bread. They do not live on this planet just to wait for a trip to heaven. They are to influence communities from within, to fill the earth with the Word of God. They are on earth as royal representatives of Christ's kingdom.

People in the world respect the purity and integrity of people who follow Christ's principles. Even if they do not verbalize it or admit it, discerning individuals recognize believers as benefits to society. On the job, employers know they can trust Christian workers. In politics, Christians maintain high personal integrity. In the business world, financiers notice a Christian's honesty.

Throughout history, Christians have been responsible for ridding society of offensive, cruel, and inhumane practices. They were responsible for ending the gladiator games in Rome. They sought the favor of ancient world rulers to end human sacrifice, polygamy, child labor, and cannibalism. Their efforts helped to end slavery and slave trading in the Western world and to establish the moral and social equality of women. From the start, they have upheld the duty of ministering to the poor and sick. Early Christians were ambassadors of their invisible King to their cities.[42]

Likewise, in this generation, saints are to be light, leaven, and a positive influence. Many Christians think the world is hopeless. They have concluded modern culture is "going to hell in a handbasket." They wonder, "Why try?" "Let's just drop out and represent Christ in hiddenness," they say. "We'll criticize and pronounce judgment on the world and wait for the rapture." But that is not their mission. They are Christ's ambassadors. He has no one else!

VISION FOR THE CITY

Most of the world's population lives in cities. Mankind lives in a network of interconnected cities with support communities in between. God loves people and is committed to reaching cities full of people. Because God is concerned about cities, His people must see them the way He does. Saints must have vision to see why God has placed them in and near cities. Vision for the local church includes vision for the city. The so-called giants of faith had vision for their cities:

Abraham   Before the Lord judged Sodom, He spoke with Abraham. Abraham had a prophetic understanding of Sodom and interceded — pleaded — for the city. Abraham was the friend of God and had God's heart toward people. God could count on Abraham to have the right attitude. Abraham could have thought, "I hope the Lord destroys Sodom; I hate that city." If he had harbored that attitude, God would not have come to him.

> And the LORD said, "Shall I hide from Abraham what I am doing, ... Because the outcry against Sodom and Gomorrah is great, and because their sin is very grave." *(Gen. 18:17, 20)*

Joshua   When Joshua sent spies to Jericho, they could have concluded that taking the city was simply too hard. They could have asked God for an easier city, one with smaller walls and fewer obstacles. Instead, they believed God could give them the city and brought back a favorable report. The Lord gave them the city.

Nehemiah   After hearing about the sad state of his own city, Nehemiah fasted, prayed, and mourned. Then he received permission to work on its restoration.

> And they said to me, 'The survivors who are left from the captivity in the province are there in great distress and reproach. The wall of Jerusalem is also broken down, and its gates are burned with fire.' So it was, when I heard these words, that I sat down and wept, and mourned for many days; I was fasting and praying before the God of heaven *(Neh. 1:3–4)*

Paul   When he saw Athens was wholly given to idolatry, Paul's spirit was grieved. The city's serious need for Christ stirred Paul to go to Jerusalem and Rome, also.

Now while Paul waited for them at Athens, his spirit was pro-
voked within him when he saw that the city was given over to idols.
(Acts 17:16).

When these things were accomplished, Paul purposed in the Spirit,
when he had passed through Macedonia and Achaia, to go to
Jerusalem, saying, "After I have been there, I must also see Rome."
(Acts 19:21)

Jonah   Jonah hated Nineveh and the people of the city. He refused to preach there. He hated the Assyrians for the crimes they repeatedly committed against his own people. The Lord ordered Jonah to preach in Nineveh, but he tried every way he could to keep from it. He knew God was merciful and would forgive if people repented. That was exactly what Jonah wanted to avoid. He wanted them to be judged and destroyed. Finally a big fish transported him there and he was forced to preach to the city. As a result, the city's 600,000 inhabitants repented and turned to the Lord in one of the greatest revivals in history. God spared the city, and Jonah got angry at God. He sank into despair. He did not have God's heart toward the city.

Jesus   Jesus had a benevolent vision and attitude toward Jerusalem. He knew He would be rejected and crucified by the city's inhabitants, yet He wept over the city. The word wept does not just mean Jesus became sad and teary-eyed. It means He sobbed and sobbed over the city. He had great compassion for Jerusalem, the very compassion of His Father. He said:

O Jerusalem, Jerusalem, the one who kills the prophets and stones
those who are sent to her! How often I wanted to gather your chil-
dren together, as a hen gathers her chicks under her wings, but you
were not willing!
(Matt. 23:37)

You did not know the time of your visitation.　　　　　*(Luke 19:44)*

The citizens of Jerusalem missed their day of visitation and Jesus wept over them. He could have said, "Because you rejected me, I will cast you off," but that was not His heart. He loved the city because He loved the people who lived there.

Believers must adopt Christ's attitude. They must have God's heart of love for their own city and the people in it, no matter how much crime, violence, and corruption occurs there. The believer's mission is to reach his city with the Gospel of Jesus Christ, and the Lord is committed to it. He will send His Word to every believer who has a prophetic vision for the city and will lead him in the mission.

And they shall call them The Holy People, the Redeemed of the
LORD; and you shall be called Sought Out, a City Not Forsaken.
　　　　　　　　　　　　　　　　　　　　(Isa. 62:12)

If Christians do not love their city, they will not reach it. God will not be able to speak to them to reveal His plans for people there. Their negative attitudes will keep them from being a dynamic presence there.

Several years ago, a young man took a liking to my second daughter. One evening my wife and I took them to dinner downtown. We sat in a restaurant overlooking the city and talked about the vision the Lord had given us for it. After dinner we stood together in the night air, and this young man made the mistake of his life. We had just said how much we loved the city and how glad we were that Portland was our city when he said, "Well, it's sure not mine!" Quickly my daughter turned and stared at him — I knew he had lost her. She loved the city and had a vision for it. She had little appreciation for a negative attitude toward it.

Once a pastor in a beautiful city with beautiful people told me, "This city is too hard. The cost of living is too high. It's too expensive to build and we can't even afford to rent a facility. And besides, the people are only interested in having a good time. They aren't interested in God in this city." The pastor had no vision for his city. I confronted him about his negative attitude, but he insisted the city was too expensive, too hard, and hopeless. He just knew that nothing would ever happen in his city. Guess what? Nothing happened in that city, and that man is not there today. In fact, he is not in the pastorate anywhere.

A true New Covenant community will have vision for the city. The Lord places churches in specific cities to pray, to be influential, and to be a blessing. If the hearts of people in a city can be changed, the city will be changed. The earth is the Lord's, and that means every city is the Lord's. Learn to confess, "This city is the Lord's," and to mean it wholeheartedly. Without that attitude, the church is really saying, "Go ahead, Devil, take this city. We don't want it. It's yours!"

To most people, the world is comprised of family and friends, but the world is larger than that. God loves people all over the whole world. Jesus gave His life for the world. To be prophetic people in the world, Christians must not isolate themselves in their own little corner of it. If believers spend all their time and energy taking care of themselves, not caring whether the world around them goes to hell, then they will stop being a prophetic people. The Bible does not say Christians are to hide in a corner and perfect one another until Jesus comes. God places people in cities to be light and salt. He wants them to reach out to others with love and care. He wants them to pray for city government and to be part of the solution to the city's problems.

> *And seek the peace of the city where I have caused you to be carried away captive, and pray to the LORD for it; for in its peace you will have peace.*   (Jer. 29:7)

Those from among you shall build the old waste places; you shall raise up the foundations of many generations; and you shall be called the Repairer of the Breach, the Restorer of Streets to Dwell In. (Isa. 58:12)

Christians have a message of hope — not judgment — for the city. Christians are redemptive agents. They are to serve, not damn.

Speak comfort to Jerusalem, and cry out to her, that her warfare is ended, that her iniquity is pardoned; for she has received from the LORD's *hand double for all her sins.* (Isa. 40:2)

THE CHURCH IN THE CITY

God sees one kingdom community in the city. He sees one church — the entire body of Christ — with many congregations. He sees the multi-membered body on a larger scale *(1 Cor. 12:12)*. Each congregation has a unique mission, message, personality and destiny.

Unique mission   Every local church has a unique, God-given vision, calling and purpose. Each congregation must be allowed to fulfill its mission without comparing it to other churches' missions.

Unique message   Each local church has dominant themes and distinctives. When all the themes and messages of congregations in a city are combined, the whole kingdom community is represented. Local churches need one another to present a unified message.

Unique personality   Every local church has a unique personality. No congregation is ideally suited for everyone, but all the congregations, when seen as a complete community, can encompass anyone and everyone. Other churches must not be judged just because they are different.

Unique destiny   Each local church has its own divine destiny. God ordained a specific time of visitation for the city of Jerusalem, and He planned unique destinies for the seven churches of Asia as follows:

- Ephesus had an apostolic church known for its hard work for the Gospel, but it tended to lose its motivation of love.

  I know your works, your labor, your patience, and that you cannot bear those who are evil. And you have tested those who say they are apostles and are not, and have found them liars; and you have persevered and have patience, and have labored for My name's sake and have not become weary. (Rev. 2:2–3)

- Smyrna had a persecuted church that maintained a faithful witness in its city.

  I know your works, tribulation, and poverty (but you are rich); and I know the blasphemy of those who say they are Jews and are not, but are a synagogue of Satan. (Rev. 2:9)

- Pergamos had another persecuted and faithful church, but it did not pay enough attention to doctrine.

  I know your works, and where you dwell, where Satan's throne is. And you hold fast to My name, and did not deny My faith even in the days in which Antipas was My faithful martyr, who was killed among you, where Satan dwells. (Rev. 2:13)

- Thyatira had a church known for its loving and serving spirit but equally known for an inattention to character.

> *I know your works, love, service, faith, and your patience;*
> *and as for your works, the last are more than the first.*
>
> *(Rev. 2:19)*

- Sardis had a church with a good reputation but no present dynamic.

> *I know your works, that you have a name that you are*
> *alive, but you are dead.* *(Rev. 3:1)*

- Philadelphia had a small church with an aggressive missionary vision.

> *I know your works. See, I have set before you an open*
> *door, and no one can shut it; for you have a little*
> *strength, yet you have kept My word, and have not denied*
> *My name.* *(Rev. 3:8)*

- Laodicea had a wealthy church that lost its zeal.

> *I know your works, that you are neither cold nor hot.*
> *I could wish you were cold or hot.* *(Rev. 3:15)*

Vision must focus on cities. God's plan began in the Garden of Eden, but it ends in a city *(Rev. 21:2)*. Churches need to lift themselves out of self-centered spirituality. They must not be ingrown or stagnant. They must have a vision-centered spirituality that looks ahead. Each generation and its leaders cannot just maintain the vision of the past. They must move on.

MULTIPLICATION YIELDS FRUIT

In His final instructions to the disciples, Jesus had said to be filled with the Spirit and then go preach the Gospel to every nation.

But you shall receive power when the Holy Spirit has come upon you; and you shall be witnesses to Me in Jerusalem, and in all Judea and Samaria, and to the end of the earth.　　(Acts 1:8)

Go therefore and make disciples of all the nations, baptizing them in the name of the Father and of the Son and of the Holy Spirit, teaching them to observe all things that I have commanded you.
(Matt. 28:19–20)

Go into all the world and preach the gospel to every creature.
(Mark 16:15)

The New Testament church was a living, growing organism. Evangelism was the core of its ongoing witness. It reproduced daily. The life of God flowed through it making it fruitful. Men and women were saved in a continuous, ongoing harvest.

Everywhere the disciples went, they preached the good news of the lordship of Christ. Multitudes were converted. The church in Jerusalem grew from 120 to 3,000 on the first day. After a notable miracle in the temple precinct, the number grew to about 5,000 men, plus more women and children.

However, many of those who heard the word believed; and the number of the men came to be about five thousand.　　(Acts 4:4)

There may have been as many as 15,000 members of the church at that point. The numbers became so great they were referred to simply as multitudes.

And believers were increasingly added to the Lord, multitudes of both men and women.   *(Acts 5:14)*

Finally, church growth changed from addition to multiplication.

Then the word of God spread, and the number of the disciples multiplied greatly in Jerusalem, and a great many of the priests were obedient to the faith   *(Acts 6:7).*

Then the churches throughout all Judea, Galilee, and Samaria had peace and were edified. And walking in the fear of the Lord and in the comfort of the Holy Spirit, they were multiplied.
                                                 (Acts 9:31; see also v. 42)

And the hand of the Lord was with them, and a great number believed and turned to the Lord.   *(Acts 11:21; see also v. 24)*

Now when the congregation had broken up, many of the Jews and devout proselytes followed Paul and Barnabas, who, speaking to them, persuaded them to continue in the grace of God.   *(Acts 13:43)*

The Great Commission cannot be ignored. A local church today wishing to have New Testament church dynamics in corporate life will evangelize aggressively. Without reproduction, a church becomes sluggish, loses vision, loses heart, and passes away within a few generations.

The church is called to take the city. It must not give the city to the forces of evil but must be an influence for righteousness. Every city has a key, although it may not be easy to find. The Lord uses keys to reach cities.[43] For example, consider the following:

- **Jerusalem.**   Harvest in Jerusalem was sparked by prayer and an outpouring of the Spirit.

However, many of those who heard the word
believed; and the number of the men came to be about
five thousand. (Acts 4:4).

- **Samaria.** Philip preached Christ to the Samaritans with signs following.

  Then Philip went down to the city of Samaria and
  preached Christ to them. And the multitudes with one
  accord heeded the things spoken by Philip, hearing and
  seeing the miracles which he did. For unclean spirits,
  crying with a loud voice, came out of many who were
  possessed; and many who were paralyzed and lame were
  healed. And there was great joy in that city. (Acts 8:5–8)

- **Lydda.** Peter ministered healing to Aeneas and got the attention of everyone in the area.

  And Peter said to him, Aeneas, Jesus the Christ heals you.
  Arise and make your bed. Then he arose immediately. So
  all who dwelt at Lydda and Sharon saw him and turned
  to the Lord. (Acts 9:34–35)

- **Antioch in Syria.** Preaching by immigrants from the Jerusalem church reached Antioch.

  But some of them were men from Cyprus and Cyrene, who,
  when they had come to Antioch, spoke to the Hellenists,
  preaching the Lord Jesus. And the hand of the Lord was
  with them, and a great number believed and turned to
  the Lord. (Acts 11:20–21)

- **Antioch in Pisidia.** The Jews rejected the Good News but the Gentiles were glad to receive it.

  > *On the next Sabbath almost the whole city came together to hear the word of God. Now when the Gentiles heard this, they were glad and glorified the word of the Lord. And as many as had been appointed to eternal life believed. And the word of the Lord was being spread throughout all the region.*   *(Acts 13:44, 48–49)*

- **Thessalonica.** Systematic, persuasive teaching in the synagogue reached the Thessalonicans.

  > *Then Paul, as his custom was, went in to them, and for three Sabbaths reasoned with them from the Scriptures, explaining and demonstrating that the Christ had to suffer and rise again from the dead, and saying, 'This Jesus whom I preach to you is the Christ.' And some of them were persuaded; and a great multitude of the devout Greeks, and not a few of the leading women, joined Paul and Silas.*   *(Acts 17:2–4)*

- **Corinth.** The Lord promised Paul a harvest of many people in the city.

  > *Now the Lord spoke to Paul in the night by a vision, "Do not be afraid, but speak, and do not keep silent; for I am with you, and no one will attack you to hurt you; for I have many people in this city." And he continued there a year and six months, teaching the word of God among them.*   *(Acts 18:9–11)*

- *Ephesus.* The Lord showed a variety of wondrous miracles to reach Ephesus.

> *This became known both to all Jews and Greeks dwelling in Ephesus; and fear fell on them all, and the name of the Lord Jesus was magnified. And many who had believed came confessing and telling their deeds. Also, many of those who had practiced magic brought their books together and burned them in the sight of all. And they counted up the value of them, and it totaled fifty thousand pieces of silver. So the word of the Lord grew mightily and prevailed.* (Acts 19:17–20)

The first New Testament churches impacted their cities. They identified with the cities, took on the strongholds of the cities, and waged valiant warfare. New Testament church members were overcomers in their generation. They were bright lights shining in the world. By the end of their generation they had preached the Gospel throughout the length and breadth of the Roman Empire. The church of Jesus Christ was built wherever they went.

Today, God stirs Christians and church leaders with vision and passion to restore the dynamics of the New Testament church in this generation. He strengthens them to be overcomers, triumphant in the places where He plants them. He is giving His church a vision for cities. He is sending His Word to His people and visiting them by His Spirit for a purpose.

Jesus said, *"I will build my church, and the gates of hell will not prevail against it"* (Matt. 16:18). Can He do it in this generation? Can He do it in your city?

The time has come to begin praying and believing God for the restoration of the dynamics of the New Testament church. He will build His church according to His pattern, and His church will prevail!

✠

STUDY QUESTIONS

1. What is the first calling of New Testament church members?

2. How did the grace of God in the church affect the relationship of believers to their community?

3. What does it mean for the church to be the light of the world?

4. In what way are Christians leaven in the world?

5. How does God respond to cities?

6. How should the people of God relate to cities?

7. How does the local church relate to the city?

8. How does this relate to evangelism?

9. What are the walls around cities?

10. What are some keys to breaking down those walls?

NOTES

CHAPTER ONE

1. R. C. H. Lenski states, "Here we have a brief description of the religious life of the first Christian congregation. All the essentials are present and are in proper order and harmony. The church has always felt that this is a model" (*The Interpretation of the Acts of the Apostles,* Minneapolis: Augsburg, 1934, p. 117). I. Howard Marshall wrote, "... the book of Acts was intended as an account of Christian beginnings in order to strengthen faith and give assurance that its foundation is firm" (21). "Luke is concerned to offer a picture of the life and worship of the church no doubt as a pattern to provide guidance for the church in his own time. [Narratives] are presented as models for Luke's readers to use. [His intent was] to show the Christians of Luke's day what it means to be the church and how they should continue to live according to the pattern established in the early days" (*The Acts of the Apostles,* Grand Rapids: Eerdmans, 1980, pp. 32–33). David John Williams commented, "It is a feature of Luke's method ... to intersperse his narrative with little cameos of life in the early church, intended no doubt, as models for the church of his own day" (*Acts* Hendrickson, 1985, p. 59).

2. Historians agree that until modern times people thought of the beginning of something as containing its pattern. The Romans

referred to the difference between *antiquitas,* early times, and *modernus,* modern times. "In all respects the concern was expressed that the present should not manifest any discontinuity with *antiquitas.* Renewals were welcomed only if they were a return to *antiquitas*" (Adriaan H. Bredero, *Christendom and Christianity in the Middle Ages,* Grand Rapids, MI: Eerdmans, 1994, p. 58). This reflected their philosophy of history and their vision of where history (and mankind) was heading. It was the more modern *Enlightenment* that changed the traditional thinking. Now the ideal is what is before us, not where things started. Mankind is progressing toward his perfection, not looking to a past pattern. To quote Bredero again: "For the Christian, the passing of time is not thought of primarily in terms of a cyclic process, but rather in terms of a final event, for both the individual and society. Humanity and the human world are *en route* toward God. In the 'post-Christian' world this belief was secularized into faith in progress" (p. 62).

3. AN AGE-OLD DEBATE has taken place concerning the exact nature of the book of Acts and how to interpret it. This is particularly true as it pertains to pentecostal theology. Most recently two eminent New Testament scholars, both pentecostal, have rehashed the arguments. Gordon D. Fee has repeated the argument that although there is theology in the writings of Luke, because "it is cast in the form of historical narrative," the principles used in interpreting that literary genre are to be used. That means that "The use of historical precedent as an analogy by which to establish a norm is never valid in itself." In other words, doctrine can be illustrated but not taught in a historical narrative. (See both "Acts — The Problem of Historical Precedent" in *How To Read the Bible for All Its Worth* [Grand Rapids, MI: Zondervan, 1982] and "Hermeneutics and Historical Precedent — a Major Problem in Pentecostal Hermeneutics" in *Perspectives on the New Pentecostalism* [Grand Rapids, MI: Baker, 1976]). William W. Menzies has countered with the view that, "The genre of Acts is not merely historical, but also intentionally theological." In his journal article "Synoptic

Theology: An Essay on Pentecostal Hermeneutics" he said, "Luke, in
furnishing a description of the early Spirit-energized church, takes
considerable pains to picture how the first community of faith came
to understand the New Era which had dawned upon them" *(Paraclete*
13.1). In other words, Luke was teaching doctrine by illustrating how it
was originally lived out in the life of the first generation church.

Many of the commentators seem to agree with Menzies.
According to F. F. Bruce the purpose of Acts must be seen in the
light of *Luke 1:1–4*; it is an apologetic as well as a historical narrative
(Commentary on the Book of the Acts, Grand Rapids, MI: Eerdmans,
1954). See also the commentary of I. Howard Marshall: "If the Gospel
gave the facts about the ministry of Jesus, Acts demonstrated how the
preaching of Jesus as the Christ corroborated and confirmed the facts
recorded in the Gospel; when the good news was preached, the Spirit
made the word effective and brought the hearers into the experience
of salvation. ... the book of Acts was intended as an account of
Christian beginnings in order to strengthen faith and give assurance
that its foundation is firm" *(The Acts of the Apostles,* Grand Rapids, MI:
Eerdmans, 1980, p. 21)

4. A. T. ROBERTSON, *The Acts of the Apostles,* vol. III in the *Word
   Pictures in the New Testament* (Grand Rapids, MI: Baker Book
   House; © Sunday School Board of the Southern Baptist Conven-
   tion, 1930) p. 34

5. CHARLES B. WILLIAMS, *The New Testament in the Language of the
   People* (Chicago, IL: Moody Press, 1937, 1966, 1967)

CHAPTER TWO

6. ALTHOUGH BAPTISM IS an important part of the Christian foundation
   it has been a source of controversy since the early second century.
   There have been several sources of controversy:

   A. How old should someone be before they are baptized? Early
      in the second century water baptism was redefined to mean

the washing away of all sins committed before the time of
baptism. Salvation then clearly required baptism. While some
chose to wait until they were on their deathbed before being
baptized others chose to baptize their infants. When Christianity became the official religion of the state infant baptism
became the norm. Then baptism became an authority issue
as well as a covenantal issue. However some maintained
the New Testament understanding and practice of baptism,
i.e. believer's baptism. If water baptism is the outward covenantal sign of true repentance and faith then a person must
be old enough to have demonstrated true repentance and
faith before being baptized.

B. How much water should be used in baptism? At the beginning of the second century sprinkling or pouring was allowed
during times of famine. This eventually became the norm.
Although there is nothing magical about the amount of water
used it seems as though immersion serves to best demonstrate the meaning of baptism, including the word "baptism" itself.

C. What verbal formula to use in baptism. Jesus had commanded his disciples to baptize believers *"in the name of the
Father and of the Son and of the Holy Spirit" (Matthew 28:19)*.
However in the book of Acts we see them baptizing *"in the
name of Jesus Christ" (2:38)*, *"in the name of the Lord Jesus" (8:16;
19:5)*, and *"in the name of the Lord" (10:48)*. Lenski pointed out
that "baptism seals us with this name and revelation and gives
us all this name and this revelation contain, and by receiving
baptism we accept it all." It has been noted that the name
of the Lord Jesus Christ is the fulfillment of the name of the
Father, Son and Holy Spirit *(cf. Acts 2:36)*. Lightfoot theorized
that the Jewish believers baptized "in the name of Jesus"
while the Gentiles baptized "in the name of the Father ..." In
this way they made it clear that Jesus was the Messiah. How-

ever, in the second century this began to result in a trinitarian controversy known as "Sabellianism" or "modalism," denying that there were three persons in the Godhead. Rebaptism was also required for those who had not been baptized with a very specific formula. All of this seemed to miss the point of water baptism and was unnecessarily divisive. (To avoid controversy perhaps we should use both formulas.) No matter what your views on these specific issues always keep in mind the covenantal nature of baptism, and don't let it become an unnecessary source of division, for there is *"... one Lord, one faith, one baptism" (Ephesians 4:5).*

7. I. HOWARD MARSHALL, *The Acts of the Apostles* (Grand Rapids, MI: Eerdmans, 1980) p. 81.

8. SINCE THE TEACHING of Charles Parham at the turn of the century, there has been controversy concerning the specific nature and experience of the baptism in the Holy Spirit. The first distinctive of "classical pentecostal" theology is that the baptism in the Holy Spirit is of necessity separate from and subsequent to the new birth. The second distinctive of pentecostal theology is that the initial physical evidence of the baptism in the Holy Spirit is only speaking in tongues. I have written more on this subject in *The Holy Spirit Today* (Portland, OR: Mannahouse Resource [formerly Bible Temple Publications], 1976, 1990). For example:

"Whether the baptism in the Spirit takes place at conversion is really not the final question, since it often happens that a person may repent, be baptized in water, and receive the Spirit all in the same day. This is, in fact, the Bible's idea. *(Acts 2:38–39; 19:2 —* 'when ye believed' literal rendering). This is what actually took place at both Pentecost and the household of Cornelius. ... [R]eceiving the Spirit is generally subsequent to repentance, water baptism and remission of sins *(Acts 2:38–39).* Ideally, it is what we might call *a distinct aspect of the conversion experience;* just as distinct as repentance or water baptism. The reason that this ideal does not occur more is due to a lack of teaching,

leadership, or practicing the Word as it is written. We are not taught
by Bible example to send people through a long probationary period
before baptizing them in water, nor should we expect them to tarry
for long periods before receiving the Spirit. On the contrary, they are
to be baptized and receive the Spirit immediately by faith and on the
basis of Christ's righteousness" (p. 39).

"Tongues are the Scriptural evidence that one has been filled
with the Holy Spirit. [The baptism in the Holy Spirit] was 'sense
perceived,' not just an invisible and mysterious operation of the Spirit
in the human heart. It was both 'seen' and 'heard' *(Acts 2:33; 10:45–46)"*
(p. 47–48).

9. CATHOLIC BIBLICAL ASSOCIATION of America, *New American Bible*
(Washington, DC: Confraternity of Christian Doctrine, 1970).

10. RICHARD FRANCIS WEYMOUTH, *The New Testament in Modern Speech:
An Idiomatic Translation into Everyday English ...* 3rd ed., edited and
revised by Ernest Hampden-Cook (Boston: The Pilgrim Press, 1909).

11. *THE JERUSALEM BIBLE* (New York: Doubleday and Company, Limited., 1966).

CHAPTER THREE

12. THIS SUMMARY IS taken from Bill Scheidler's excellent book, *The New
Testament Church and Its Ministries* (Portland, OR: Bible Temple Pub-
lications, 1980), pp. 48–50.

CHAPTER FOUR

13. FREQUENTLY IN THE history of the church, renewal movements have
advocated a radical break with the "institutional church." By that they
have always meant a break with church authority — both those who
are in authority and the structure of authority itself. Our generation
has been no exception. A recent example has presented itself. The
so-called "Open Church Movement" has been proposed by James

H. Rutz and described in his book, *The Open Church* (Auburn, MA: SeedSowers, 1992). There are many excellent principles and exhortations in Rutz's book, but it is also possible to see the classical, tragic and unnecessary **overreaction** against authority. Here are just a few examples:

> "Encourage your men to become leaders by spearheading new satellite congregations. That's clearly a Biblical pattern. As they create these new fellowships, have them bear in mind the example of ... owning no buildings, keeping no membership data, and hiring no professionals" (p. 35).

> "[The modern-day] all-in-one pastor is a *not-quite Catholic priest!* ... there is not one verse of Scripture in the New Testament that describes [a pastor], and only one verse that even uses the term 'pastors' *(Ephesians 4:11)*" (p. 68–69).

> "*There must be no appointed leader in these home meetings.* What goes on inside those home meetings must not be organized. NO designated leaders. None! And only the barest instruction of what to do in those home meetings. *Minimum instruction*" (p. 80).

> "There should be someone in all gatherings (not someone considered to be a leader, but just an ordinary peasant) who is designated to end the meeting" (p. 89).

> "*If the God-appointed leaders of your church will not even agree to study and pray about having an open church, rejoice!* What comes next in your life may be the most breathtaking event of all: an opportunity for you to pioneer a whole fresh, new matrix of fellowship" (p. 97).

> "*If, in the sovereignty and timing of God, your church board flat-out refuses to allow a restoration of the three freedoms: open worship, open sharing, and open ministry ... refuses to allow an alternative service ... and even refuses to allow an open mini-church within their structure ... you still have one excellent*

> *option left:forming a whole new church — an open church — as*
> *a mission project or daughter church"* (p. 102).
>
> *"If you want to revert to the exact scriptural pattern, you'll*
> *have to dissolve the pastorate, dynamite the sanctuary, and do a*
> *whole long list of others things ..."* (p. 106).

14. I HAVE WRITTEN at length on this subject of team ministry. If you
would like to look into it more may I refer you to *Team Ministry:*
Putting Together a Team That Makes Churches Grow (Portland, OR:
Mannahouse Resource [formerly Bible Temple Publications], 1984).

15. FRANK DAMAZIO HAS written an excellent exposition on the role of the
senior elder in *Effective Keys to Successful Leadership* (Portland, OR:
Mannahouse Resource [formerly Bible Temple Publications], 1993).

16. COMMENTARIES ON THE Johannine epistles agree with this interpretation of *Third John* and this description of the development of local
church authority at the end of the first century. For instance, in the
excellent *New International Commentary on the New Testament* series,
I. Howard Marshall wrote, "Its background [*3 John*] appears to lie in
the growth of a new type of church organization. At first the various churches were to a considerable extent under the guidance and
leadership of apostles and evangelists ... who traveled from place to
place and maintained a general supervision over the churches placed
under their care. In this type of situation, the role and authority of the
local leaders whom they appointed was correspondingly restricted,
but as time passed and churches increased in number, a new situation
began to arise. The apostles and their colleagues were growing old, or
had actually died. There was no defined universal system of succes-
sion, and it was natural that local churches should begin to develop a
more powerful leadership of their own. At the same time, there was
a tendency toward the concentration of leadership. In the early days,
church leaders constituted a group of elders or of bishops and deacons. Now this 'team ministry' was giving way to the idea of one man
as the bishop who occupied a position of leadership over the other

officials" *(The Epistles of John,* Grand Rapids, MI: Eerdmans, 1978, pp. 10–11).

17. LET ME REFER you again to Bill Scheidler's excellent work, *The New Testament Church and Its Ministries.* Bill gives a fairly exhaustive treatment of the ministry of the apostle. On page 91 he summarizes it this way:

   A. The apostle will be involved in founding and establishing the Church on a proper foundation. *1 Cor. 3:9–14; Eph. 2:20; 1 Cor. 9:1–2; 11:34.*

   B. The apostle is one who will be particularly concerned about doctrinal exactness. *Acts 2:42; 15:1–31.*

   C. The apostle will have the signs of an apostle accompanying his ministry. *Rom. 15:18–19; 2 Cor. 12:12.*

   D. The apostle may be involved in Church discipline at times, particularly in relationship to the Church he has founded. *Acts 5:1–11; 1 Cor. 5.*

   E. The apostle is involved in the ordination of ministries such as elders and deacons. *Acts 6:1–6; 14:23; Tit. 1:5.*

   F. The apostle is involved in the feeding and training of other ministries. *2 Tim. 2:2.*

   G. The apostle is to be involved with caring for the Churches which he has begun. *2 Cor. 11:28.*

   H. The apostle is used in presbytery, in the laying on of hands and the impartation of spiritual gifts. *1 Tim. 1:18; 4:14; 2 Tim. 1:6; Rom. 1:11.*

   I. The apostle is not a dictator *(1 Cor. 16:12),* nor a lord over the sheep *(1 Pet. 5:2),* but as a father he is to help the members of the body of Christ come to maturity *(1 Cor. 4:15–16; 2 Cor. 1:29).*

18. CHURCH HISTORIANS SEEM to be united in observing this pattern of the institutionalization of local church leadership at the beginning of the second century. The writings of Ignatius of Antioch c. 107 are an excellent example. The historical term for the local bishop was "monarchical bishop" and the regional bishop the "diocesan bishop."

For more details see the standard *Christianity Through the Centuries: A History of the Christian Church* by Earle E. Cairns (Grand Rapids: Zondervan, rev. 1981), pp. 115–117, and *The Story of Christianity, Volume 1: The Early Church to the Dawn of the Reformation* by Justo L. Gonzalez (New York: Harper & Row, 1984), pp. 62–66, as well as Gonzalez' *A History of Christian Thought. Volume 1: From the Beginnings to the Council of Chalcedon* (Nashville: Abingdon, rev. 1987), pp. 71–80.

19. THE LOCKMAN FOUNDATION, *The Amplified Bible* (Grand Rapids, MI: Zondervan Corp., 1987).

CHAPTER FIVE

20. LENSKI COMMENTED, "THIS work went on continuously, and all these people not only attended the meetings faithfully but also earnestly adhered to what was taught."

21. WILLIAM F. BECK, *The New Testament in the Language of Today* (Saint Louis, MO: Concordia Publishing House, 1963).

22. KENNETH N. TAYLOR, *The Living Bible* (Wheaton, IL: Tyndale House, 1971).

CHAPTER SIX

23. F. F. BRUCE, COMMENTARY *on the Book of the Acts,* (Grand Rapids: Eerdmans, 1954), p. 80.

24. R. C. H. LENSKI, THE *Interpretation of the Acts of the Apostles,* (Minneapolis: Augsburg, 1934) p. 117.

25. ROBERT YOUNG, YOUNG'S *Analytical Concordance to the Bible,* revised, corrected (Nashville, TN: Thomas Nelson Publishers, 1982), "Concordance" p. 768, *s.v.* PRAYER; "Index-Lexicon" p. 49, *s.v.* TEPHILLAH.

26. H. W. F. GESENIUS, GESENIUS' *Hebrew-Chaldee Lexicon to the Old Testament,* translated by S. P. Tregelles (Grand Rapids, MI: Baker Book House Co., 1979), pp. 871–872, *s.v.* הָלְכָת.

27. THE LOCKMAN FOUNDATION, *New American Standard Bible* (Grand Rapids, MI: Zondervan Corp., 1977).

CHAPTER SEVEN

28. THE ACTS OF *the Apostles* by I. Howard Marshall. *The Tyndale New Testament Commentaries,* vol. 5, Wm. B. Eerdmans (Grand Rapids: MI, 1980), p. 84.

CHAPTER EIGHT

29. IN HIS COMMENTARY *on the Book of the Acts, (The New International Commentary on the New Testament),* Grand Rapids: Wm. B. Eerdmans, 1954, p. 80. R. C. H. Lenski also comments, "... they considered and treated their possessions, not as belonging to the owner only, but as something in which the rest were to share as need arose." *The Interpretation of The Acts of the Apostles.* Minneapolis: Augsburg, 1934, p. 118–119. I. Howard Marshall adds, "... each person held his goods at the disposal of the others whenever the need arose." *The Acts of the Apostles. The Tyndale New Testament Commentaries*, vol. 5. Grand Rapids, MI: Wm. B. Eerdmans, 1980, p. 84.

CHAPTER NINE

30. IN THE DYNAMICS *of Corporate Gathering* (Portland, OR: Bible Temple Publishing, 1990), Frank Damazio lists seven aspects of a true New Testament covenant community:

 A. "Covenant community exists when people are more concerned with the corporate local body than with themselves. Corporate life becomes more important than the individual's own pleasure or will.

    B. "Covenant community exists when individuals are being knitted, built, framed, and joined together. This speaks of close, long-lasting, real friendships.

    C. "Covenant community exists when the spirit of sacrifice becomes the attitude in which the community meets the needs of all.

    D. "Covenant community exists when people want to spend time together in both spiritual and natural activities.

    E. "Covenant community exists when the elderly retain proper godly authority throughout their lives and are cherished and respected by the community.

    F. "Covenant community exists when the family is in biblical order: the husband or father taking his rightful place as head of the home; the wife finding fulfillment in this atmosphere; the children well-disciplined, happy, and secure.

    G. "Covenant community exists when humanism, selfishness, independence, and isolation are treated as intruding viruses. They are overcome and destroyed by applying the Word of God so that covenant community may become a reality" (pages 11–12).

31. The Lockman Foundation, *The Amplified Bible* (Grand Rapids, MI: Zondervan Corp., 1987).

32. Msgr. R. A. Knox, *The New Testament of Our Lord and Saviour Jesus Christ: A New Translation* (New York: Sheed & Ward, 1945).

33. William Barclay, *The New Testament: A New Translation* (London: William Collins Sons & Co., Ltd., 1968, 1969).

34. Joint Committee on the New Translation of the Bible, *New English Bible* (New York: Oxford University Press, 1970).

35. J. B. Phillips, *The New Testament in Modern English*, revised (New York: Macmillan Publishing Co., 1972).

36. According to F. F. Bruce's *Commentary on the Book of the Acts,* "the believers met regularly in the temple precincts for public worship and public witness, while they took their fellowship meals in each other's

homes" (p. 81). He went on to say that "the community was organized along the lines of the voluntary type of association called a *havurah*, a central feature of which was the communal meal. The communal meal could not conveniently be eaten in the temple precincts, so they ate 'by households.'"

37. IN *THE OPEN Church,* James Rutz claims that the early church met only in homes. For him the restoration of the church involves returning to the living room. However this is not only contrary to the clear record of history but is, more importantly, contrary to the pattern of Scriptures. For example:

> "In the biggest blunder in her history, the church began constructing lots of buildings, displacing the catacombs and forest glens — and ending forever the warm, precious, meetings in someone's living room" (p. 10).
>
> "That which we know as the Christian faith was a living room movement! The Christian faith was the first and only religion ever to exist that did not use special temples of worship; it is the only 'living room' religion in human history" (p. 55).

38. BILL SCHEIDLER HAS written a training course for small group leaders. In it he lists a seven-part vision for small groups:
    A. To care for all of the needs of the flock, *Ps. 23:1; Jer. 23:4.*
    B. To raise up strong marriages and families, *Mal. 4:6.*
    C. To bring each person to a place of personal maturity, *Eph. 4:13.*
    D. To foster strong inter-personal relationship among the sheep, *Eph. 4:16.*
    E. To assist and equip each person in finding and fulfilling their place of ministry, *Eph. 4:11–12.*
    F. To be available to each member of the body for counsel, support, encouragement and comfort, *Ps. 23:3.*

G. To gather lost sheep and integrate them into the flock,
   Eze. 34:12–16.

He also gives a four-part purpose for small groups:

A. Pastoral care and discipleship. The home meeting approach is a biblical way of feeding a multitude of people.

B. Building relationships and fellowship. The home meeting will help to keep people from being alone in the midst of a large number of people.

C. Assimilating new people into the church. It takes several years to feel a part of a crowd, but in a few brief contacts in an intimate setting, people can feel loved, cared for and needed.

D. Evangelism.

39. W. E. VINE, *VINE's Expository Dictionary of the Old and New Testament Words*, volume 4, edited by F. F. Bruce (Old Tappan, NJ: Fleming H. Revell Co., 1971), p. 35, *s.v.* SINGLENESS, APHELOTĒS.

CHAPTER TEN

40. *THE EXPOSITOR's GREEK Testament* comments that this was "characteristic of their whole devotional life both in public and private; and their life of worship and praise, combined with their liberality and their simplicity of life helped to secure for them the result given in the following words ..." (W. Robertson Nicoll, ed., Vol. II, Part I, "The Acts of the Apostles," R. J. Knowling, Grand Rapids: Eerdmans, p. 98).

41. J. B. PHILLIPS, *THE New Testament in Modern English*, revised (New York: Macmillan Publishing Co., 1972).

42. I. HOWARD MARSHALL commented, "As the Christians were seen and heard by the other people in Jerusalem, their activities formed an opportunity for witness" *(The Acts of the Apostles.* The Tyndale New Testament Commentaries, vol. 5. Grand Rapids: Wm. B. Eerdmans, 1980, p. 86). *The Expositor's Greek Testament* added, "The pure and simple life of the disciples doubtless commended them to the people, and made it easier for them to gain confidence, and so converts. ..."

43. FRANK DAMAZIO'S EXCELLENT book *The Vanguard Leader* (Portland, OR: Mannahouse Resource [formerly Bible Temple Publishing], 1994) elaborates on this theme. I recommend you read chapter 5, "The Strategy: Taking the City".

✠

CPSIA information can be obtained
at www.ICGtesting.com
Printed in the USA
BVHW042324150223
658636BV00021B/282